The Working Woman's GPS

When the Plan to Have It All Has Led You Astray

JJ DiGeronimo

ISBN Paperback: 979-8-9856897-0-9
ISBN Electronic: 979-8-9856897-1-6
Library of Congress Control Number: 2022904369

Editor: Deborah Burke and Patricia M. Gerkin
Cover Design: Patty Penca
Cover Photo: JenniferAnne Photography

Published by Together We Seek Publishing
Printed in the United States of America.

JJ DiGeronimo
JJDiGeronimo.com

To our daughters, nieces, future daughters-in-law, and granddaughters.
May our wisdom, sacrifices, and accomplishments aid your success.
Blaze the trail that is your own.

OTHER TITLES BY JJ DIGERONIMO

*Accelerate Your Impact: Action-Based Strategies
to Pave Your Professional Path*

*Seeking: 74 Key Findings to Raise Your Energy, Sidestep Your
Self-Doubts, and Align with Your Life's Work*

*Illuminate Your Path: How Life's Crossroads Awaken the Gifts
You Already Carry. 6 Phases of Spiritual Awakening*

CONTENTS

PART IV:
REFOCUS, RECALCULATE, ACCELERATE

So, I Was Told . . .

by society, my culture, the women's movement, my school, and my family that if I worked hard I could have it All: fabulous career, great spouse, wonderful family, financial freedom, success, friends, hobbies, philanthropy, and time for community activities. Can you relate?

So I set my sights on that direction. My burning desire to achieve the All drove me in the direction of perceived success. I accomplished many of its promises, yet as I checked off each prerequisite needed to get it All, I was surprised that I didn't feel the happiness I had envisioned and expected. Sometimes there were notable external celebrations, like wine, a nice dinner, an award, but it was not the formalized and distinguished observances I had expected. Internally, I didn't feel fulfilled.

I strive to be a successful working woman, wife, mother, sister, friend, and daughter...and more. But I was misguided about the sense of fulfillment I expected. Instead of feeling excited and overjoyed by my accomplishments, having it All left me overcommitted, exhausted, and detached, with many life threads tangled. I felt foreign in my own skin. Even after all my efforts, I still seemed short of the goal.

After much reflection, I learned to create new expectations and a new destination for my journey, which include Goals with a sense of Purpose and Self (GPS). I redefined what I thought would work for me. Then I asked other successful business women to share stories from their journeys as they too evolved from what was expected of them to what inspired them. As working women, we had many points where our life choices and their consequences intersected. Often, I found we shared similar triumphs. I discovered that many women also found it necessary to step back, make new choices, discover new sources of energy, and re-frame their lives.

This book captures the journeys of working women who daily manage many priorities. As smart, strong, and savvy women, we continue to strive for success—and also for balance and harmony—in every priority, every choice, and every opportunity that comes our way. We have become wiser as we've learned from our life experiences and choices.

Have you too arrived at this point, or do you hope to? As you've worked harder and taken on more responsibility, have you realized your choices have taken you to an unknown destination?

If you're looking for clarity and a route back to an "inspired" you, let's figure out the problem and how it started. Let's re-examine what we are striving for and why. Let's determine what we need to release, what we can give, and what we need to keep for ourselves. Then let's take off in the direction of our fulfillment.

Together, let's envision and become women who live lives of inspiration.

JJ DiGeronimo

PART I:
THE PLAN TO HAVE IT ALL

CHAPTER 1

My Story

Before you agree to do anything that might add even the smallest amount of stress to your life, ask yourself: What is my truest intention? Give yourself time to let a yes resound within you. When it's right, I guarantee that your entire body will feel it. ~**Oprah Winfrey**

As I approached the age of thirty, I was soaring in the high-tech world after graduating from college eight years earlier with a degree in computer science. I loved the pace, the people, and the evangelistic role of next-generation technology, which allowed me to travel, learn, and grow. I had a good life and amazing work experiences that took me from Brazil to Germany to the UK and back to California. I was eager to advance my career and I thrived on the energy. Many of my non-work hours were spent enjoying the outdoors, traveling with close family and friends, and taking care of myself by working out, reading good books, and enjoying great food and engaging conversation.

Yet, it became apparent that I was missing what I thought was a very important piece in what I call the "Plan to have it All," that map to success that society encouraged women to follow. Although I had many wonderful partners, I was yearning for a life partner—someone who would grow along with me, so we could push each other ahead, and stabilize each other when needed. As I traveled the world, I would spend some of my airport time visualizing the relationship I wanted; I made lists of the qualities I wanted in my life partner. Like many motivational authors encourage, I stated what kind of life partner I wanted. I stated it *out loud*, and then I gave my wish-list to the Universe.

When he first appeared at a friend's wedding, I didn't give him much thought. He was charming, enjoyable, and engaging, but he lived in Ohio and I lived in Georgia. I wasn't eager to move, and he was involved in a business that required him to stay in Ohio. We continued to meet on weekends, and it seemed so easy—I felt like I had known him for years. As the months went by, we shared our life goals and aspirations; the synergy was magical.

After our engagement, I was eager to move to be near him. Since my job required me to travel, I was confident that I could maintain my life and career even with a move. So I packed my bags and landed in his hometown in Ohio. I laugh now, but as I drove my life possessions in my SUV up Interstate 71, I had no clear idea of what an impact this choice would have on my life. I only knew it was part of the Plan. Isn't that what we do? We make the choices we think will make us happy. I was delighted to have found such a wonderful life partner and happy to check off another prerequisite for having it All. I was headed for the altar.

Months after I unpacked in Ohio and the wedding bells stopped ringing, I felt I had made a huge mistake—

not with my choice in a life mate—but with my surround-
ings and the unspoken pressures that fell on me as an Ital-
ian wife in a small suburb.

Then the high-tech company that employed me was
bought by Yahoo!®. I was offered a similar job, but the job
required me to travel more than 75 percent of the time. I
loved my work, but after ten years on the road I had had
enough of planes, rental cars, and hotel rooms.

Eager to get into another exciting technology role, I
began searching for a comparable job in Ohio that would
require less travel but still bring the excitement of high
tech, big cities, and emerging leaders. That combination
was close to impossible to locate quickly with the slim
Rolodex of contacts I had in my new city. Although I could
not find a comparable job, I forced myself to find "a" job.
At the time, I didn't realize that the wrong job would add
an additional level of frustration.

My new situation seemed overwhelming, but I kept
pushing forward. After a few months, I began to notice
how frustrated I had become. Upon reflection, I felt disappointed in myself for making so many changes in such
a short period of time: getting married, moving to a new
city, finding a new job, adding new pressures. I heavily
weighed leaving my marriage. It seemed that one choice
had turned everything else upside down. I loved my husband, but I was out of my comfort zone in the city where
he lived. Horrified, I watched my career regress.

To make matters more challenging, my husband had
an overwhelming desire for a child, which I immediately
resisted. I had even more internal discussions about leav-

ing my marriage. I felt torn, and I knew I was ill-equipped in my present state to handle yet another demand and another change. I recognized that my choices had turned my internal harmony upside down, and I was eager to get back on track. I didn't want to make yet another decision—to become a mother—on top of all the other decisions I had made. It wasn't that I didn't want to be a mother; I just wasn't ready to handle motherhood at that time. Although it seemed like a natural progression to get married and have a child, I felt I had lost my inner compass. My energy sources had evaporated—all because of my "good" choice.

My individual choices may have made great sense at the time, but I could not seem to harmonize them with other choices. The life threads I cared so much about become more and more tangled.

I was lost and overwhelmed: some people didn't notice, and those who did couldn't understand why. After all, I was married to a wonderful man, and I had much more than the basics in life.

Was this the "Plan to have it All?" I wondered. If so, why did I feel so disconnected from myself, so empty?

And this is when I began to revise my plan and to redefine my journey . . . .

CHAPTER 2:

The Working Woman's Dilemma

Perhaps too much of everything is as bad as too little.
~Edna Ferber

If you, too, are a working woman (or have had a career and now choose other ways to spend your time), you know that life is all about choices. Each choice has consequences. The choices we make daily do not reside in a vacuum; rather, they often have an impact on multiple areas of our lives. Many choices are automatic: we sense they are "expected." For example, we are expected to show up at work every day and do an excellent job; expected to provide love and care for our families; expected to pay our taxes. The better we are at achieving the expected results, the more we are asked to achieve. Expectations pile upon expectations. Sound familiar?

"I can't do the laundry," Shelley, forty, tells me. "I can't keep everything clean. The mundane stuff has to be done. The lunches need to be packed and the backpacks need the snow pants in them and the extra shoes in them, the homework needs to be done and the spelling words need to be tested and the baths have to be done and the hair needs to be combed. It's just insane. There's no end to all that I need to do. And my husband has all this free time. And I don't know how he gets this free time. You know what he asks me? He asks me why I don't make time for my hobby and invest in my own pottery wheel, have a pottery shop, and make my own pottery. I don't have enough time to *go* to a pottery class let alone to actually think I could do pottery and sell it. And the kids don't understand that when mom has a conference call they have to be quiet and it takes precedence over playing Candy Land. They don't get it."

Women born in the mid-to-late 1940s through the present day have been told by our culture—by advertising, business, society, and the school systems—that we can "have it All" in terms of ideal partner, wonderful motherhood, spectacular career, success, money, and happiness. It's "All" available.

As women of the twenty-first century, we are bombarded with cultural and societal expectations that many of us have chosen to adopt as our own personal goals. We were taught to believe in the Plan; it has been pitched to us since childhood. We based our life choices on it, because, after all, the Plan to have it All seemed like such a grand thing, didn't it? Society expects us to fulfill the Plan's requirements and we expect it of ourselves.

Many of us bought into the promise of the Plan without realizing it. We learned about the Plan through many overt, as well as subliminal, messages. The Plan, at least in part, is the source of our drive and ambition. Yet, following this Plan has often resulted in our confusion and despair.

Crickett, fifty-nine, has had a number of careers, first traveling worldwide to emerging markets, before being promoted to vice-president of divisional merchandise with a large department store, when department stores were starting to create private labels.

When Crickett became an executive buyer and began traveling, her boss came up to her one day. Crickett shared their conversation:

"Crickett, you don't have children do you?" her boss asked.

"No," Crickett answered.

"Because if you did," her boss looked at her, "I would tell you that there are no excuses."

"That was the attitude," Crickett explained. In other words, if Crickett wanted to have it All, children could not be used as an excuse for any kind of work absence.

"I was pretty certain I wanted to have kids, I just didn't know when," Crickett said.

When the department store was closed, Crickett faced that choice.

"I was thirty years old and I had to choose whether to have children or to go on to another department store," Crickett said. "And I chose to have a baby."

When Crickett left the company, she learned that she had received substantially less pay than men in comparable positions because, her company argued, "You have a husband to support you."

Cathy, forty-nine, was one of the few women I spoke with who said she never entered her professional life thinking she could have it All. "I thought I needed to balance my home and my work life, particularly by delegating things that I didn't need to touch personally, so I didn't go insane," Cathy told me.

The Working Woman's GPS:
When the Plan to Have It All Has Led You Astray

Cathy went into law. As a young lawyer, she couldn't help but notice that professional women frequently had to leave business meetings because their children were sick. She said there was an unspoken but strong sense that professional men in the company had a derogatory opinion of women who left work for sick children or stayed home with sick children: they were not reliable, couldn't be counted on to work late, and had their priorities "screwed up." These women didn't make partner.

As a result, Cathy waited until she was older and had made partner in her law firm before she had children. "I saw what happened to women who didn't," she told me.

What exactly is the Plan and how did we learn about it? Why did some of us go after it so fiercely, and sometimes to our detriment? Having it All is subjective. The Plan may have unfolded for you in a different way than it did for me.

The Plan has been operative in the life of every woman I've spoken with. For many of us, the Plan required difficult choices that created unexpected situations that then required even more difficult choices. The Plan affected most of our choices around those gifts most dear to us: children, family, husband, career, community, and philanthropy. These are the lovely colored threads that give our life meaning. Haven't we all had to admit that it's tough to keep all the threads of life smooth and untangled?

Many of the women I've interviewed eventually created their own Plan and set forth on their own individual path, which was a result of the roadblocks they encountered in the Plan they had been following. They found their own path after taking many wrong turns suggested by the Plan and finding themselves at a dead end.

I spoke with Leah, a thirty-two-year-old wife and mother of two, who describes herself as a "sassy Korean-American professional, an Innovator, Fashionista, and Foodie. Maybe even a little weird." I asked her if she felt pressured to achieve and have it All.

"The women's movement put more pressure on us," Leah said. "Yes, we can be powerhouses in the workforce, but we also have to be a good wife, we have to look good all the time, we have to be sharp all the time."

Is there a working woman who hasn't felt this way?

Shelley, forty, who admitted she couldn't do all the mundane stuff, is a software expert in high-tech. She and I shared a ride to the airport recently. She asked me what I thought about being a working Mom, and she wondered how I managed to keep it all together. I laughed, pulled out my tape recorder, and told her about this book. It only took a minute for her to accept my invitation to tell her story. I started the interview with, "Are you happy?"

"Some days I'm happier than on other days," Shelley said. "I wanted it all; I got it all. I got the family I wanted: I have two girls. I got the property I wanted, the house I wanted, the husband I wanted. I got a job pretty much exactly what I wanted. . . . So I have it all, but am I happy? No. I can't do it all. It's too much. There's no way."

"In our society, it is extremely difficult to balance the guilt of managing being a working mother and having a career," said fifty-two-year-old Sharon, who had had many kinds of jobs, including fashion merchandising, lactation consultant, and health food store owner.

The Working Woman's GPS:
When the Plan to Have It All Has Led You Astray

Often, we don't realize that our lives are too busy or that we've made a choice, or a series of choices, that has complicated life. Nothing seems to harmonize, and we wonder why. We're left exhausted, frustrated, and wondering: How did I get to this point? Is this what I was expecting my life to be? Am I happy?

Let's take "happy" and examine it for a moment. After spending hours interviewing working women, it dawned on me that I really don't know what "happy" means. It may be too vague, too subjective. The same is true for other words women often mentioned, such as "balance" and "perfect." After reflecting on these words, I've realized there are better, richer words that may get to the crux of our distress with the Plan, words like inspiration, energy, and focus. We'll take a closer look at these words, and how they relate, later in the book.

Through my own journey, I've learned that striving to have it All isn't all "champagne and caviar". Sure, there were moments of joy—and even more moments of disappointment—as I struggled to keep focused on the promise of success and happiness held out by the Plan. I've worked the Plan as well as I could. I've come to realize that this one-sized Plan does not fit all; many of us have found it defective.

It's important to clearly name the expectations you fulfilled; the choices you made; the problems that resulted; and the challenges you still face because you've followed the Plan to have it All. What twists and turns did you encounter as a result of choices that seemed to make sense at the time? Consider the questions below as a starting place:

- When do you remember first hearing about the Plan to have it All?
- How did the Plan manifest in your life?
- What dilemmas resulted from your choices?
- Name the roadblocks (obstacles). Be as specific as possible.
- Did women in your life give you any advice about the Plan?
- If you've reached the oasis of having it All, how does it feel? Is it what you expected?
- Are you inspired by the life you've created?

CHAPTER 3:

The Plan's History & Current Obstacles

Woman must not accept; she must challenge. She must not be awed by that which has been built up around her; she must reverence that woman in her which struggles for expression. ~**Margaret Sanger**

Ambition and success are not bad; they are not the ogres in our story. But we need to admit to the life situations our choices have created. Often, we don't realize that our lives are too busy or that our choices have created more problems than we can handle until we are so immersed in our life decisions that we assume that altering direction is nearly impossible.

Obstacles are often opportunities in disguise, so I don't treat them as negative energies. What we call "detours" happen most frequently when we are overworked, over-committed, or find ourselves in an undesirable situation. If these terms apply to you, consider them clues. You may be receiving clues about your next growth edge: you may need to make alternate choices, give yourself permission to let go of some things, or take time to redefine your goals and choices. Try to view these clues as messengers.

The Working Woman's GPS:
When the Plan to Have It All Has Led You Astray

Think of all the threads women hold: partner, family, children, career, friends, community, hobby, self. It's nearly impossible to keep them all from tangling. Think of the roles we play: spouse, mother, employee, daughter, sister, friend, caretaker, housekeeper, supporter, carpooler, and more. We are expected to interweave all the threads without getting them tangled and to intermingle all our roles without getting them confused. Daily, we're forced to make difficult decisions that ultimately sacrifice one or more threads and override one or more roles. Why?

I think we have these problems because we bought into the Plan to have it All. This Plan seems real.

It wasn't that long ago that a much different Plan was operating. Some of our grandmothers and great-grandmothers had different expectations placed on them by the culture and society of their day. Their Plan for happiness and fulfillment involved just two items: marriage and motherhood.

Of course, some of these women worked very hard in business; maybe one of your courageous ancestors was ahead of her time. Clearly, many of our mothers and grandmothers were working women who made extraordinary contributions to their families, communities, and the world. Some of them were no doubt part of the women's liberation movement that helped introduce the Plan we have now. This new Plan erupted on the American stage in the early 1960s.

The women's liberation movement—or feminism—insisted that a woman's legal, political, and social rights were equal to those of men.[1] Although feminism may seem out of date to younger women, it's important to understand that it has had a critical influence on our lives.

It took the first group of early feminists seventy-two years to obtain women's right to vote (1848 to 1920). We owe the privileges we have today to the women who came before us. I will return to this theme later as I believe we have a responsibility to our daughters and nieces, to our sons, and the generations that come after us to offer a new vision, to change what is and isn't working in our lives, just as the women before us worked to change the inequality that prevented them from achieving their full potential.

This is by no means an exhaustive history of the women's movement, but rather a selection of events. These events have influenced those of us who have tried to have it All.

In the 1960s, the women's liberation movement was instrumental in changing our legal and social rights. The Plan that now runs most of our lives began to take shape in 1963, when Betty Friedan published *The Feminine Mystique*, which questioned the then-current plan for a woman's happiness. The book discounted the widely held belief ` that marriage and motherhood fulfilled all of a woman's needs. Friedan's book set the burgeoning women's movement afire. By 1966, the National Organization of Women (NOW), which began with twenty-eight members and a budget of $140, influenced women all over the United States. Within four months, membership grew to three hundred and the budget grew to $1,500. According to the

---

NOW website (www.now.org), the organization currently has 500,000 contributing members and 550 chapters in all states and the District of Columbia.

During the '60s and '70s, NOW was instrumental in establishing courses in women's studies at many universities including Princeton--courses never even considered in earlier generations. In 1969, New York University Law School offered the first accredited law course for women, while other schools delayed. During a 1971 congressional hearing on discrimination against women, Rep. Martha Griffiths (D-MI) testified that Virginia state schools had turned down 21,000 women for admission, while refusing no man who applied. The Professional Women's Caucus sued every law school in the United States that discriminated against women and still received federal funding.

NOW successfully introduced and passed child care legislation, which helped women with children enter the workforce. The efforts of the women who came before us cannot be underestimated. They worked to tap the potential in all women, honor women's gifts, and change the lives of women and men.

For example, a 1965 survey of female graduates at Stanford University found that 70 percent of those women did not plan to work at all when their children were under six years old, and only 43 percent said they would work when their children turned twelve or older.

Yet, by 1972—just seven years later—female graduates of Stanford gave much different responses to the same survey questions: fewer than one out of every twenty-five women graduates expected to be full-time homemakers.

Women were beginning to think differently about what was important to them.

They were beginning to read books like *The Feminine Mystique,* Juliet Mitchell's *The Longest Revolution* (1966), Evelyn Reed's *Feminism and the Female Eunuch* (1971), and Erica Jong's *Fear of Flying* (1973), and to re-think their attitude toward their lives. They still loved their husbands and children, but now, grasping their own amazing potential, they wanted a chance to see what they could do.

Cigarette companies began exploiting the women's movement. Ads for Virginia Slims used catchy phrases, such as "You've come a long way, baby." Television, newspaper, and magazines all promoted the Plan. By 1978, women were expected to be hard-working, sexy, and sophisticated employees who also did everything expected of their grandmothers in terms of marriage and motherhood.

Women kept fighting for an end to sex discrimination. More than one hundred women from women's liberations groups invaded the office of that stalwart magazine, *Ladies' Home Journal,* and conducted an eleven-hour sit-in to protest the magazine's portrayal of women as well as the hardships of the magazine's female employees.

Women of that time were "roaring"—singer Helen Reddy chose the right word in her famous 1970 song "I am Woman."[2] Women all over America and in cities around the world were protesting inequality and marching for the freedoms we enjoy today. Sometimes they were jailed, beaten, or fired from a job for their views and actions. And sometimes their views led to divorce. But they earned for us what we have today: opportunities for success unavail-

---

2   *Helen Reddy, I Am Woman, (Helen Reddy and Ray Burton, songwriters) 1970.*

able to women in the past. We've come far because the women before us were brave and effective change agents.

A few more brief stories about how the women's movement changed society are worth mentioning here. The editor of the *Washington Post* issued a 1970 memorandum to the newspaper's staff stipulating that reporters could no longer refer to women in their articles in terms such as "cute," "brunette," or "divorcee"—unless they used similar terms to describe men.

Employers nationwide, stunned by the number of women standing up for themselves, agreed to stop referring to women as "girls."

NOW members worked diligently for Title VII of the Civil Rights Act of 1964, which prohibited sex discrimination in employment hiring. The Act was passed, but inequality remained. The Equal Opportunity Employment Commission, which was created to enforce the Civil Rights Act, voted to permit sex discrimination in job advertising. As recently as forty years ago, women like us worked under a culturally sanctioned cloud of discrimination. In 1978, after a nationwide outcry by women, Congress outlawed discrimination in the workplace based on pregnancy.

With the number of women holding top political offices today, it's easy to forget that political roles were not always open to women. The 1960s was a transformative decade as more and more women ran for political office. Margaret Chase Smith became the first woman to be elected to both the U.S. House and the Senate. She was also the first woman to run for the presidential nomination of a major party. At the Republican Convention in San Francisco in 1964, Smith received twenty-seven delegate votes, more than anyone else except the eventual Republican nominee, Barry Goldwater. In 1972, Rep. Shirley Chisholm was the first African-American woman to run for the U.S. presidency in the primary of a major political party. Chisholm was known for her outspoken honesty. NOW endorsed her candidacy for president and worked tirelessly to organize her campaign in many states.

After being elected to the House of Representatives in 1978, Geraldine Ferraro was the first woman to represent a major political party as a vice-presidential candidate in the 1984 election.

Women were being selected for posts previously held by men. Dr. Juanita Kreps became the first woman to hold the position of U.S Secretary of Commerce, holding that office from 1977 to 1979 under President Jimmy Carter. Kreps was also the first woman board member of the U.S. Stock Exchange.

In 1917, there was one woman in the House of Representatives and no women in the Senate. Today, during the 111th Congress, there are seventy-seven women in the House of Representatives and seventeen women in the U.S. Senate. Representation of women in Congress is at an all-time high of 17 percent. Women are now expected and encouraged to run for political office. Women have had a long, uneven, and painful journey to equality in the marketplace.

This graph from the Bureau of Labor Statistics (Fig. 1) shows the astounding rise in the number of working women over the last fifty years. Most working women I've spoken with are grateful for their job and career opportunities. The women who came before us made it happen.

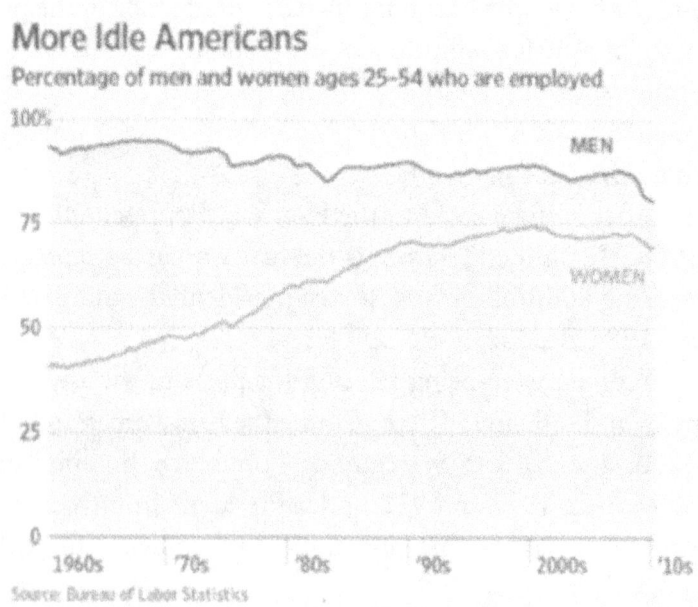

More Idle Americans

Percentage of men and women ages 25-54 who are employed

Fig. 1: Employment Trends

As we know, true equality still eludes us. The 2008 U.S. Census figures reveal that the median income annual earnings of women fifteen and older who worked full time and year round was $35,745, down from year-round, full-time earnings of $36,451 in 2007 (after adjusting for inflation). Women earned seventy-seven cents for every one dollar earned by men.[3]

---

3   *Income, Poverty, and Health Insurance Coverage in the United States: 2008. http://www.census.gov/*

Recent U.S. Labor statistics reveal that women are still underpaid in jobs comparable to men. Most career women have experienced this firsthand. *Forbes* magazine published a recent list of highest-paid CEOs in the nation's five hundred largest companies. The first woman came in at number forty-eight. This speaks volumes in a country where women make up 47 percent of the workforce, yet only 3 percent of Fortune 500 CEOs are women. Sadly, nearly fifty years later, women's equality in the workplace is an ongoing effort.

The United Nations Department of Economic and Social Affairs report *The Millennium Development Goals Report 2007,* stated that "worldwide more than 60 percent of unpaid family workers are women," meaning that women in many developing nations continue to lack access to job security and social protection. The UN Educational, Scientific and Cultural Organization (UNESCO) reports that forty-three million girls worldwide are still denied a primary education. Two-thirds of the 137 million illiterate young people in the world are women. In Afghanistan, there are thirty- six literate young women for every one hundred literate young men.

We may not be able to quickly change the cultures of other countries, but we can be aware of—and make small steps toward advancing—women all over the world.

History holds important lessons. This incomplete history of the women's movement provides the context for the Plan we have today. Just as the women before us had challenges to address, so do we. As they did not shrink from their challenges, neither must we. We can learn from the women's movement and the women who emerged, faced their challenges, and made the world better for us. Now it's our turn.

The Plan's Criteria

The Plan now in vogue consists of a series of choices that, once made—and *correctly* made—have the potential to make us successful, inspired, and fulfilled. Society and our culture say so!

The choices at the heart of the Plan include, but are not limited to, education, marriage, children, career, and financial and material security. One woman's life can hold all or some of these choices. Some choices are individually tailored, such as if you marry and whom you marry, or if you have children, when and how. Financial goals and community involvement may be important to some women and not important to others.

Sarah M., thirty-four, has been in health care for the past thirteen years and is currently focused on Business Integration. She is also a mom to two girls. When we talked, Sarah told me that she is definitely trying to fulfill the Plan to have it All. When I asked her what "having it All" means, she said: "If I could describe it in one word it means *balance*, in terms of feeling like I'm giving enough of my time to my children so that they can have it All, so they can have true happiness. That I'm giving enough to my husband so that he feels fulfilled in our marriage and I feel fulfilled in our marriage. And enough time to myself so I can do what I want to do in life, whether it's working out, having enough time to read, or having a career. Having it All is summed up for me in the word *balance*."

"Do you feel balanced?" I asked her.

"No," she said.

"Why not?"

"Probably because of the choices I make. I choose to put more of my time and energy into work, whether it be worrying about it or putting time into it. Most of my choices are between family and work and I put less time into myself. I don't feel balanced with myself."

I've felt this way, and every woman I've talked to has experienced this inner imbalance. Having it All seems like an illusion precisely because it keeps eluding us. The truth is, we *can't* do everything required to have it All. The equation is somehow faulty.

I don't think that the Plan handed down to us is about achieving balance, whether inner or outer. That's a problem. And it isn't about living a life of energy and enthusiasm, a life that inspires us and others. That's a problem, too.

The best part of the Plan we operate under today is that we have the power to modify it, to create a more effective life—a life with impact. We have the power to redefine the Plan so that our sons and daughters, nieces and nephews, young friends and neighbors will one day thank us for bringing more energy, focus, and inspiration into the lifetimes we've been given.

CHAPTER 4:

Is the Plan Working for You?

*If a plant cannot live according to its nature,
it dies, and so does [a human being].* (adapted)
~Henry David Thoreau

Leah asked me—and by extension, all of us—a rhetorical question: "Do you want it all? I mean, really? Do you really want it All?"

She echoed a question I've heard from many women—including my own inner voice. And this: Is what I have achieved the "All" I really want?

Why am I here? each of us has asked at one time or another. We begin to ask, What is my life's purpose? We come to these deep questions at different ages and under assorted circumstances, but invariably the questions find us. When we become aware of such questions, we are likely to pause and consider them.

Since we learn from our choices and their consequences, it's important to re-assess our choices on a regular basis. We may just need to change our attitude; sometimes we need to change our direction. Such changes are not always easy or comfortable.

Life is a school and earth is our school house—we are here to learn. I realize now that the hardest parts of my life were my best teachers; they helped me progress in greater self-awareness and self-understanding. The difficult parts helped me focus my energy and develop greater inner harmony; the tough road is not to be denied or run from, but embraced as a true gift. I can honestly admit that disappointment, betrayal, and failure helped me understand myself more than did my successes and achievements.

I think this is what happens: we need the hard parts to show us who we truly are. Difficulties prompt us to ask the tough questions, and the honest answers keep us on our toes and challenge us to be more than we thought we could be.

Usually it happens this way: One day while we're driving the kids to school, preparing a customer presentation, daydreaming at the gym, or emptying the dishwasher, those tormenting questions suddenly hit. How did I get here? Am I happy? Who am I? What IS my purpose?

Paulette, sixty-two, lives in Massachusetts with George, her husband of forty years. She retired as vice-president of a huge telecommunications company, and she currently works as an entrepreneur.

Paulette was married and came into the marketplace in the early 1970s at the time when the Plan for women as we know it was getting into full swing.

"When I started," she told me, "the focus on the workplace was just starting. It was easier for me to get promoted because people were looking for someone like me. I know I was good; it was easier (than now) to be identified."

Paulette broke rank with the women in her family who had gone before her. She and her husband decided together not to have children right away, deciding instead to concentrate first on their careers. Paulette achieved great success, a success much different than that of her parents.

"There were two men in my life who were significant to me," she said. "The first was my father. I was the oldest of three. My father attained his GED in his sixties. He constantly pushed me, my brother, and sister that college was a given. He never graduated from high school. He was always there for us to encourage us and pushed us to excel.

"The other person who was influential," she continued, "was my husband. He was from a family of six and when we first got married, he absolutely wanted me to live through my potential. . . . The way we wanted to approach things was that we would *both* do *both*. We wanted to excel in our careers but not so much that we couldn't both excel in having a family."

Eight years after marrying, Paulette and George began their family. They had two sons. Once she had children, Paulette found going to work painful.

"Oh my God, I was torn," she says. "I still remember that time like it was yesterday. I would say that for the first twenty-five years of my career I was never sure I was going to stay [with my company]. I was never sure I was going to be a working mom."

"Where do you think that came from?" I asked.

"My mother was a stay-at-home mom. So my immediate models weren't what I was doing. My focus was to do it 'All.'"

We know that when we work full time, care for a family, tend to parents, friends, and interests, and try to live fully, we become exhausted.

I asked Paulette, "What kept you going to work for twenty-five years?"

She chuckled. "I didn't know this at the time but I sure knew this when I retired. It became clear what it did to me. As an individual and as person, I needed the reinforcement associated with what I got at work. I was challenged and I was successful. I received positive reinforcement and the opportunity to do things that additional financial reward allowed me to do, things that we could enjoy as a family. We bought that summer home, we bought that boat, we sent our kids to the schools we wanted to send them to, and we did many social things."

The perks from working hard and having a career are nothing to quibble with. Paulette laid them out very well: challenge, opportunities, positive reinforcement, promotions, financial reward, and emotional fulfillment.

I wanted to learn what Paulette did for herself during those years when she was a working mom. What had she done to care for herself so she could keep going?

She was silent for a moment. For the first time in our conversation, she hesitated.

"I'm not sure that fit into the mix," she finally said. "I could only work and have a family. . . During that time, I ended up gaining a lot of weight. I gave up a lot," Paulette said, "but I didn't give up my family or my profession. I gave up on myself."

That's another problem with the Plan: it requires us to give up part—or all—of ourselves in order to make other parts work. Eventually, giving up parts of ourselves becomes something we have to deal with.

Remember Sarah M., who's been in the health care industry for thirteen years? In high school, Sarah wanted to be a doctor. She earned her BS in Microbiology and began her career in Infection Control at a prestigious Midwestern university hospital cancer center and research institute doing clinical research.

"I remember feeling I had to do *everything* in order to make it, to be well rounded, and to get into the best college," Sarah said. "The message I kept hearing was 'you've got to get involved in everything, you have to be well-rounded, you have to be smart, and you have to be very philanthropic. You have got to do it All to be able to make it in medical school.'"

"What benefits do you get from working?" I asked her.

"Hmmm," she said. "Great question."

Her delay in responding was lengthy, so I reworded the question. "Why do you feel you put so many of your eggs in the work basket?"

"Probably because it's where I spend 80 percent of my time," she admitted. "I put time into it because it is measured. You know, I have not only a paycheck to measure it, but I have other measurements like my performance review and rewards trips."

"If you didn't have a paycheck, would you still be doing what you're doing?" I asked.

"No," she said, quickly.

"What would you be doing if money didn't matter?"

For the first time in our conversation, Sarah got excited. Her voice changed, even the pitch of her voice revealed her excitement. "Something truly philanthropic," she hurried to say. "Something where I felt it was making a difference in someone's life, in their well-being . . . something connected to life."

I can't presume to know, but I believe that excitement may have been Sarah's inner voice suddenly sending her a message. Through my question, I may have inadvertently brought Sarah's deeper life purpose out into the open.

Our first jobs or initial work are not always about our life purpose. This was true even for such figures as Mother Teresa and Oprah Winfrey. Each of these accomplished and philanthropic women found her true purpose later in life.

Kimberly, twenty-four, is in medical equipment sales in Chicago. I asked her how she got to where she is today and if it's where she wants to be. Kimberly told me that she graduated from the University of Illinois in 2007 with a finance degree and a minor in Spanish. She studied abroad and traveled the world. When she returned home to Chicago, she landed a job with a well-known financial institution doing corporate lending. She was there for nearly four years.

"I was definitely in a man's world, the finance world and banking, lending to Fortune 500 companies, dealing with the CEOs in giant corporations with huge egos," Kimberly said.

She experienced men as less talkative than women and better at producing. "It was definitely a battle," she said, "but I liked working with men."

Still, despite excelling, Kimberly felt out of place. "It was like a boy's club," Kimberly said of the corporate lending field. "There was an associate who was a level above me, and she, too, was often frustrated with the boys' exclusive side conversations. I did very well there," Kimberly said, "except for the fact that the men-dominated workplace was not the ideal environment for me to continue growing my career."

Kimberly evaluated her feelings, observed her energy, learned something from her experience, and made a different choice. The point is that as we notice our feelings, how our energy is increased or depleted over time, at work and at home, we will be better able to discern our true direction. Then, if need be, we can always reset our "purpose compass".

Christy, thirty-eight, was a high-powered vice-president at twenty-eight years old. When she married and began a family, things really changed. Because Christy was so successful at a young age, I wondered how she felt when she left her career, married, and began a family. Did she miss all the career perks?

"It was an identity crisis," Christy confessed. "I have always associated myself with my career. You meet somebody at a cocktail party or any place else, and the first question asked is, 'What do you do?' I've always been able to say, 'I'm a VP at this company or an executive at that company and that was a way to associate myself. It's increasingly difficult to answer that question now with 'I'm a working-from-home mom.'"

That brings us back to Leah's question: Do we really want to have it All? And back to Paulette—and many women—who gave up parts of themselves to fulfill the Plan to achieve it All in the business world.

The Working Woman's GPS:
When the Plan to Have It All Has Led You Astray

As I speak with working women, it doesn't take long before we are discussing demands, time constraints, and choices. The increased responsibilities put enormous strain on our time and our energy. We find ourselves running faster and faster to keep the Plan to have it All in motion. For some of us, the Plan is our operating system. It's how we execute our lives. We don't dare fall short of the expectations.

As women, we know our emotions can change hour by hour, even minute by minute. As we become aware of our energy levels and observe our feelings, we gain critical information that we may not have realized consciously. I find it works best if I notice and observe without necessarily judging or acting on the information.

Take note of your energy levels and feelings without making judgments about them. In the midst of unloading the glasses from the dishwasher, when the thought, Am I happy?, appears out of nowhere, pause for a minute and feel the question. Is it in your head only? Your heart, gut, shoulders? Is it the first time you've asked that question or the fiftieth? Those eruptions of deep questions are actually very good signs. They call us to take a good look at ourselves and examine our happiness and our unhappiness, to take responsibility for our lives. Just be aware of them, and then go on putting the glasses in the cupboard. This kind of self-questioning and self-reflection can only help us take the next step in redefining the Plan for our individual lives, for rediscovering our true purpose.

Maybe there are better ways to prosper than by overextending, overworking, and overdoing. Whether working mothers or not, we seem to be struggling with the Plan to have it All. If that dream is eluding us in some way, is there another more important dream waiting?

When my inner voice protested about how hard I was trying to make everything work at home and at work and in my world, it didn't quit. It kept haunting me, whispering in my ear, shouting, leading me a little further in the journey. I had to take stock of where I was and explore how I got there. I had to ask myself if there were pieces of myself I lost along the way.

Let's work to refocus, re-energize, and become inspired again for ourselves, our families, and our world. Let's find ways to make the impact we were meant to make—not because of what we *do*—but because of who we *are*. Running so fast so much of the time, we sometimes, accidentally, run off course. The difficult questions that erupt in us are clues that help us reset our "purpose compass."

So, if you've worked the Plan and you're not inspired, or if the current Plan has led you off course, it's time to take an inventory to assess your current position. Knowing your current location, you can more effectively program in new information to get you back on the road toward a life that is full of inspiration.

PART II: INVENTORIES– MARK YOUR STARTING POINT

CHAPTER 5:

Why Inventories?

You take your life in your own hands, and what happens?
A terrible thing: no one to blame.
~**Erica Jong**

We have power to change our journey and the responsibility to evolve. As the saying goes—a journey of a thousand miles begins with a single step.

But before any of us starts to accelerate, it's important to understand where we are starting from. Your car's GPS can give you directions to a new place only from your starting point. That's why we need the inventories.

Webster's gives these two definitions: 1) An inventory is a) an itemized list of current assets or b) a survey of natural resources; or c) a list of traits, preferences, attitudes, interests, or abilities used to evaluate personal characteristics or skills; and 2) the quantity of goods or materials on hand."

For our purposes, both definitions are useful.

What we inventory is our life as-is, including how we choose to fill our days. We take a look at what we have, where we are, what obstacles we've met and overcome, and those we still face.

The Working Woman's GPS:
When the Plan to Have It All Has Led You Astray

When we pull a project together, where do we usually begin? By doing an inventory of the assets, people, skills, abilities, and resources needed to complete the project, including those that are available and ready to work for us and those we yet need to gather. The same process applies here.

If you've picked up this book because some part of you is looking for inspiration to reroute your direction to a place of greater satisfaction and fulfillment, then the practices I'll describe may help. These inventories helped me when I realized that the Plan I adopted as my own was running my life into a ditch.

We usually consider change as something uncomfortable; we don't always welcome its unexpected appearance. Yet, when *we* invite change into our lives, it doesn't feel so rocky and uncertain; it feels more like a welcome adventure. As I evolved, I could see that when I made a choice for change, it was more empowering and energizing than if I waited for change to happen to me or if I made a passive choice to accept something that I did not consciously choose.

Life makes us pay attention by putting up stop signs where we used to yield. I mentioned that I was disconnected from my best self after I married and moved to Ohio. While I had breezed through other life changes, this one baffled me. I had to stop; I was unsatisfied, confused, and discouraged. That's when I began to take inventory. I wanted to understand my current location, the full scope of my situation. Looking back, it was obvious life had stopped me for a reason. Fully grasping my current location would allow me to set a path toward a new destination.

Why Inventories?

By using the inventories that follow, I came to a pivotal moment that enabled me to reset my direction in life and re-energize my purpose compass. I became more aware and eager to understand. As a result, I experienced a greater sense of inspiration and peace. These inventories allowed me to set off in peaceful confidence to a new and fulfilling destination. And I wasn't the only beneficiary: my loved ones benefited from my renewed focus. They found me more inspired, light-hearted, and purposeful, with my priorities in alignment.

Maria, twenty-six, manager in supply chain management met me for coffee one morning and expressed her desire for more in her life. I mentioned the inventories that I had recently documented for this book, and I asked if she would be interested in completing the exercises to ensure they provided the self-insight I was striving for. I asked her to provide feedback on the inventory formats and process.

Maria eagerly agreed and asked that I send the inventories that day. After a few weeks, I had moved on to other chapters, and I had forgotten that I had sent early versions to her. Then Maria left me a jovial voice message that she had completed the first two inventories.

Maria cautiously admits that, after completing the inventory, she realizes that her choices have brought her both celebration and heartache as she reflects on work, loved ones, and health. "Yet," she said, "life has made me stronger and showed me what really mattered and what I was made of. These experiences have made me realize how strong, grateful, graceful, and loving I am, which will guide me through my most challenging times."

The Working Woman's GPS:
When the Plan to Have It All Has Led You Astray

If you remember *The Gambler,* a song by Kenny Rogers,[4] I want to propose that we could adapt the words of that song in a different way; they don't have to be about gambling. Rather we can apply them to how we live. We, too, need to be aware of what to throw away and what to keep.

Everyone is dealt a separate hand in life. It's important not to play all of our cards, to fold some of them, to draw some new ones. At points in our lives we may need to fold all our cards, turn them in, and draw new ones—by altering our direction. Maybe we need to reshuffle to create a winning hand.

The inventories helped me reconnect with myself and my energy sources. They gave me a clearer idea of where I was and where I needed to go, and why. In life, we get some good hands and some not-so-good hands. No one I know has had only winning hands.

But the key is the kind of hand we choose to play. Which kind of hand do you want to play? The best poker players know that a winning hand requires critical choices. Sometimes we make the poor choice that we later regret, but that's okay, too. As I said, I believe everything happens for a reason. On our way to a life of inspiration we can use the losses as well as the successes to move us forward.

Take your life into your own hands. Look at the cards you're playing. Take an inventory and figure out what kind of hand you really want to bet on.

---

4   *Kenny Rogers, title track to 1978 album, The Gambler, which won him a 1980 Grammy for best male country vocal performance.*

CHAPTER 6

Inventory A–People & Energy

The minute you alter your perception of yourself and your future, both you and your future begin to change.
~**Marilee Zdenek**

Initially, I made the mistake of thinking I didn't need to do a personal inventory. I overlooked this crucial step, so I know you too may be tempted to leap into decisions and actions before identifying the full scope of your current situation.

I thought I had made an accurate assessment of my life, only to find that I had made some assumptions about myself, and the resources and people around me, that weren't completely true. For example, I came to realize only later that the professional and personal connections I made in my new town after I married were only reflections of how removed I was from my true self at the time. When I thought I could rely on these people, they turned out to be as phony as I was at the time. I, having lost sight of my best self, had been pretending everything was fine and ignoring my inner voice. Later, when I tried to rely on some of these people for support, they weren't available. And the truth is, neither was I.

The Working Woman's GPS:
When the Plan to Have It All Has Led You Astray

I also convinced myself that I was in a pretty steady frame of mind. If I had been honest with myself, I would have known that I was disengaged, uncomfortable in my own skin, and discouraged. Had I recognized these signs, I would have spoken gently to myself and said, "JJ, you need to 'get it together' if you want to get yourself back on track." But I wasn't honest with myself, so it took me some time to find my way. Eventually, I had a series of questionable situations and choices that compelled me to perform an inventory similar to what I'm encouraging you to do now. I hope you can avoid some of my missteps and misfortunes by working your way through these inventories first.

Be honest with yourself as you create and organize your inventory. Consider this self-inventory as important as one of your most significant projects at work, at home, or in the community. In fact, this inventory is most essential because it impacts every other aspect of your life.

The first inventory is about the people in your life. We begin here because your relationships are a view into who you think you are and what you think you deserve.

Who Do You Enjoy Being With?
Make a list of the personal and professional people you know. I like to group them by how I know them or how I interact with them: Friends, Immediate Family, Co-workers, Neighbors and Community Friends.

This is a list not only of the people you love, but those people you see on a regular basis. Think of people you would invite to a house party you are hosting; usually, we don't invite casual acquaintances to a party, although, occasionally, we may. If people don't make the party list at your home, chances are good that you wouldn't call on them in time of need. Remember, ultimately you're looking for people you can count on. If a casual acquaintance comes to mind as a person you may be able to count on, put him or her on the list. The list will likely change over time; throughout your journey, you may find yourself deleting some names and adding others.

Next to the names of people, I created a second column about how each person made me feel. I used symbols to rate—not the person—but myself: How did *I* feel when I was with that person?

Try it. It gets you right to the heart of how you feel about the people in your life. You aren't judging them; rather, you are acknowledging how you truly feel when you are with them. This is the system I use; feel free to create your own.

- (+): This symbol indicates that I feel good when I'm with this person, that I look forward to seeing him/her.
- (-): This symbol means that I rarely feel good about myself when I'm with this person; often, I feel unease when I'm with him/her.
- (/): This symbol indicates that I have mixed feelings about this person. I feel neither positive nor negative. This symbol means "it depends" on how I feel the day I see him/her, what's on my mind, or how he/she behaves. In most cases, this symbol indicates that I feel neutral toward this

person. I may need to pay closer attention to my feelings about him/her.

Initially, I made my list of people on a napkin, eventually moving it to an Excel spreadsheet so I could easily see the data. (See Figs. 2A-C)

Names	Feel
Friends (lifelong)	
Terri	+
Chris	+
Riley	/
Elizabeth	-
Rebecca	-
Immediate Family	
Mom	+
Dad	+
Brother	+
Sister-in-Law	+
Co-workers	
Todd	-
Linda	+
Nancy	/
Community Friends	
Samantha	+
Jamie	/
Sienna	-
Beth	+
John	+

Fig. 2A: People Inventory (Feelings)

Who Gives You Energy?

To get even more information about yourself, create a third column on your spreadsheet. This column measures how each person affects your energy. Use the same symbols and ask yourself: Does this person make reasonable demands on my time and energy?

- (+) I feel good energy. I like our give-and-take relationship. I enjoy this person's energy. Together, we have good synergy, which means that together we might create a dynamite new hors d'oeuvre, come up with a new direction for the project, or discover a great place to take our families on vacation. Or maybe this person and I always laugh, creating a lighter feeling in me and a deeper joy in both of us.
- (-) This person takes advantage of our relationship and asks more of me than I feel comfortable providing. She/he drains my energy.
- (/) I have mixed feelings about this person. I need to further investigate my energy level when I'm with her/him.

Doing an inventory of how people and their energies affect you is vital. We all have friends and family who have become guides for our journeys, providing friendship, energy, and feedback. Use your inner voice as a compass in addition to the people in your life who are sources of guidance.

Inventory A–People & Energy

Names	Feel	Energy
Friends (lifelong)		
Terri	+	+
Chris	+	+
Riley	/	/
Elizabeth	-	/
Rebecca	-	-
Immediate Family		
Mom	+	+
Dad	+	+
Brother	+	+
Sister-in-Law	+	+
Co-workers		
Todd	-	-
Linda	+	+
Nancy	/	/
Community Friends		
Samantha	+	+
Jamie	/	/
Sienna	-	-
Beth	+	/
John	+	+

Fig. 2B: People Inventory (Energy)

Who Supports Your Journey?

Now, go one step further. Add a fourth column using the same symbols to document answers to this question: Does this person and my relationship with this person support or hinder my journey?

- (+) Means the relationship is positive; it challenges me in a good and healthy way to be my best self. This person and my relationship with her/him is helpful to me now and could, in the future, help me progress on my journey.

- (-) Means this person, and my relationship with her/him, hinders me. It is primarily negative and critical; I feel discouraged from moving toward opportunities.

- (/) Means I'm unsure whether this person, and my relationship with him/her, hinders or supports my journey. This relationship could go either way and needs further assessment.

Names	Feel	Energy	Support
Friends (lifelong)			
Terri	+	+	+
Chris	+	+	+
Riley	/	/	-
Elizabeth	-	/	+
Rebecca	-	-	-
Immediate Family			
Mom	+	+	+
Dad	+	+	+
Brother	+	+	+
Sister-in-Law	+	+	+
Co-workers			
Todd	-	-	-
Linda	+	+	-
Nancy	/	/	/
Community Friends			
Samantha	+	+	+
Jamie	/	/	-
Sienna	-	-	-
Beth	+	/	/
John	+	+	/

Fig. 2C: People Inventory (Support)

The Working Woman's GPS:
When the Plan to Have It All Has Led You Astray

Don't be tempted to conduct this inventory in your head. You can start by thinking about the people in your life, but please put them down on paper. That's the whole point: This isn't a head exercise, it's a heart exercise. It's not about thinking about your friends and family but about noticing how you *feel* when you are around them, how they affect your energy, and your confidence, whether you think they believe in you or not. This is good information. Don't keep it in your head where you store the date, the car payment due date, and the soccer schedule. Write it down so you can study it and use it as a tool to ignite your journey.

After Maria took this inventory, she realized something: "This specific inventory was an eye-opening exercise," she wrote me. "It made it apparent that sometimes I grasped onto people because I was scared and often held on too long. This list makes it so objective. It is now more visible that some people in my life truly hold me back and drain my energy."

What will you do with this inventory? In the next section, I'll ask you to establish a support team for yourself, so it's crucial that you understand which people belong to your true support system and why you chose them.

Gillian, twenty-five, is a public relations executive. She realized how much it affected her when she and her long-time boyfriend broke up because they realized they "weren't a great fit."

"It really threw me for a loop," Gillian admitted, until she had an insight. "When I broke up with my boyfriend, it was rather liberating to think only of myself. I had to ask myself 'What do I want to do?'" Gillian realized that she now had the opportunity to know herself as an independent, successful woman.

Gillian's mother and aunts had all married early and none of them had worked steadily. Gillian followed a different path, moving to a big city and landing a great job. "Now I feel like I'm blazing a new path," she said.

She made it a point to get to know her co-workers well and to establish relationships that work in her professional life. "I'm very interpersonal," Gillian said. "I really try to forge a deeper connection than just work. I've created a work family in my professional life."

Gillian also found that "cultivating some really, really close friends" is a big help on the journey. "I've networked a group of people in Chicago that I really enjoy and trust," she said. She realized that she's learned to be strong, that she doesn't necessarily need to fulfill every piece of the Plan to be happy. "Life can be great," she said, "if you surround yourself with those you love and trust."

Sarah R., forty-five, is a single mother and an entrepreneur who is in the process of reinventing herself. She immediately knew who she felt great about, who gave her energy, and who she could count on. "My girlfriends," Sarah laughed, "my single-momma friends. There's a bunch of us. I have wonderful support from my parents as well. I'm very fortunate."

As you begin to notice your feelings around the various people in your life, how they affect your energy, and how they affect your life journey, you will likely think of other people to add to the list and some people you will want to remove—especially when you understand how they consume your energy. Although we may often do things and go places with people who do not energize us—because we've known them for a long time, it's convenient or kind, or they're "family"—removing them from your list is not necessarily removing them from your life. Of course you will continue to see these people and you still will care about them. They are not *bad* people. But they can't be part of the team you will put together.

If you put them on your team—despite their negative energy—you will likely burn out before *you* see the finish line. Add them to your team now and you'll be carrying extra baggage on your journey. When we've recognized the Plan is flawed, we'll want to lighten our load, not increase it. It's best to tell these friends that you're taking a self-inflicted sabbatical and you'll be focusing on some self-development. Focus on people who are sources of good energy and minimize daily contact with the negative- energy people, for now.

Kimberly described a woman in a senior-level position at a former company where Kim worked. It was unusual in this particular company for women to attain high positions. This woman's energy and vibe struck Kim.

"She was not your warm and friendly person," Kimberly said. She was not very approachable, with her tough exterior. I wondered if that toughness helped her land that position. I would look at her and ask myself: Is that how I want to be? Is that how I need to act to move up in the world?"

When I asked Kimberly what relationships give her energy, she knew immediately. "My family for one," she said.

"My family recharges my battery, when I go home."

"But whose energy motivates you?"

"Mostly, my Mom's," Kimberly said. "I don't know if she ingrained that [working is good] in me or if she just gave off that aura. I respect my Mom and I like what she has done with her career. She's found a way to balance it all, and I want to be just like her. She taught me the importance of maintaining a job and having an income. If you have an income, you can spend your own hard-earned money."

Kim's mother had good energy and it rubbed off on her.

What's Your Vibe?

As long as we are on people and their energy, I want to mention something about the vibration each of us gives off. Think of it as your "vibe," the energy you radiate in most situations. Watch people walk into a coffee shop, and see if you can tell who is inspired by the life they created, who is worried, who is distracted, who is starting the day with a headache, and who is relaxed. I bet you can pick up clues—we can sense people's vibe. And they can sense ours.

What is your vibe? What kind of energy do you exude? Before you ask others to share their positive energy with you, quiz yourself.

- How do I think people feel when they're around me? In general, do people enjoy being with me?
- Do I inspire the people to be all they can be?
- Do positive people lighten me? Do negative people deflate me?

- How would people rate me on their people inventory (Figs. 2)?

Along with noticing your vibe, make a point of listening to what you say and to whom. Notice your communication patterns (verbal and non-verbal) with various people. Is it enthusiastic? Lighthearted? Passionate? Is it low energy, moody, complaining? Is it always serious? When you speak to someone, do they engage you in response? Do you see a pattern in how people engage with you? What if you altered your energy a bit; might you attract a different type of person?

One day at her son's gym class, Leah sat next to a friend, and they got on the topic of self-description. Leah asked her friend, "If you had to describe me, what would you say?"

Her friend turned to her, looked her in the eye, and said, "Intense."

"Really?" Leah was shocked. "You think I'm intense?"

Her friend's assessment stunned Leah. She didn't think of herself as intense; she considered herself fun, lively, and joyful. She thought people enjoyed being around her. She thought she gave people good energy.

"That was my turning point," Leah said of her friend's assessment. "Am I intense? Yes, very much so. But the intensity my friend saw came from a strong dissatisfaction with my job. I wasn't happy. There was chaos and not enough structure. When I left work, I didn't want to do the things I loved because I had been doing them all day long.

"So my friend's comment that I was intense made me take action. It made me seek a new job that would use my gifts and challenge me by providing structure and focus. I wanted to redirect my career so that professional fulfillment would literally flow into my entire life and soften my unintentionally intense parts."

Asking our friends, family, and co-workers for their honest assessment of us may yield a few surprises, as it did for Leah. Yet Leah's surprise turned into greater self-discovery and a new direction.

We all emit positive as well as negative energy. Don't be surprised when you make some changes and the people around you ask, "What's going on with *you?*" Smile to yourself. You're making progress.

A note of caution: Take your time with Inventory A. It may take some time to assess the scope of people and energies around you. As you work through the other inventories, continue to work on this one, adding or subtracting people based on how you feel when you are with them and how their energy affects you.

With this inventory, you've dug into your actual exchanges of energies. If you've dug deeply, with breathtaking honesty, this inventory will help shed more light on the path you sense is there but may not yet see.

CHAPTER 7:

Inventory B–Assets & Resources

Sure it's easy to be upbeat when everything is going your way.
Anyone can do that. It is far more important, however,
to take a positive approach to circumstances that
most people would view as negative.
~Ralph Marston

This next inventory will give you a good idea of what you have to bring to the forefront and who can help you do it. You'll see that I'm asking you to look at these two broad topics of Assets and Resources in a new way.

What Are Your Assets?

Assets are what *you* can offer the world. They come from within you. You have been given special gifts. Do you know what they are? Make a list of your

- talents,
- skills,
- special attainments,
- awards, and
- special abilities or strengths.

Maybe you're the go-to person to help organize a space, or the plant lady neighbors come to for advice. Maybe you're a collector of special items such as rare books or coins. You may have been making doo-dads or quilts or sketches throughout your life—not knowing why. These are some of your assets. Everything counts, especially quirky talents and creative ideas.

You may have attained educational success, or received awards, special recognition, or praise for your skills at work or as a volunteer in your community. Just think, if there were no *you*, what would the world be missing?

Paulette, the former regional president of a telecommunications company, once received an award by the Minority Managers Association when she was a senior manager at her company. The award was given to a senior manager who most advanced the spirit of equality in the workplace. Then, when Paulette left the company, she was surprised to receive so many letters from people she hardly knew. One letter stuck in her mind.

"It was from a first level foreman/manager indicating how significant it was for him to work in the organization because it was the first time he felt valued and appreciated for the individual contribution he was able to make. In that letter he shared that he was a gay man; I never knew that! It was astounding to me, first of all that he was a gay man and it was incredibly reinforcing to me that I had made a difference in his life."

That would be one of Paulette's assets.

What might other people say about you? Ask the people you listed in Inventory A to describe your assets. Would they mention that ad campaign you came up with? Would they comment on that great grant you wrote or that inspiring talk you gave at a work conference? Would they remind you that you are always the go-to person when something pressing needs to be done? Would they mention that you always come into a room with a smile on your face or that you never seem to lose your temper or your patience?

If you've participated in a 360-degree feedback offered now by many companies, you may well understand how your effectiveness is viewed by others. The feedback in the 360-degree provides such insight about the skills and behaviors we bring to the organization's mission, vision, and goals. If you have not had this type of organized feedback, it may be time to ask your colleagues or your supervisor to provide one. Be curious about the responses from the 360. Focus on listening while you take notes. Don't become defensive and rebut anything they tell you. You may learn something about yourself you didn't know. Good or bad, the information is something you can build on as you evolve your Plan toward a more inspired life.

Sarah R., who is now re-entering the marketplace after staying home with her children for many years, has decided to put her emphasis on the needs of her children—they are her primary assets. She has chosen to decline many job offers that she once would have eagerly accepted.

"A lot of positions that are innate to me are not conducive to being a single parent," Sarah said. "So I have to redefine what it is that I'm going after. I've decided that I'm CEO of Simon and Sylvie, my two children, and I'm not going to get those big, fancy jobs, although I'm still attracted to them."

Sarah is also offering the world the strength of her convictions. She has chosen not to further tangle her threads because she wants her children to remain a top priority. If you clarify what you do well, note your strengths and interests, and what you take pride in, that effort alone will help you clarify the journey.

After completing the assets section of this inventory, Maria wrote me that her "assets, skills, and talents are not aligned" with her current job. "I need to make use of my special gifts," she said.

Standing up for others, voicing opinions, and prioritizing other commitments in a particular way can all be assets to list on this inventory, in addition to our natural given talents, skills, and knowledge.

I'll say it again: Inventory work is not to be rushed; sink into the work; let it speak to you.

Examples of Assets
- Leader
- Animal Lover
- Connector
- Good Listener
- Entrepreneur
- Empathetic person

What Are Your Resources?
Resources are tangible skills and things other people possess that you can access, such as money, transportation, computers, a good lawyer, a carpool partner, a potential business partner, a handyman, a great nanny, a pottery studio, a cabin in the woods. This is a very short list of potential resources. Your assets you find within you; your

resources you discover outside, in the wide world of people and possibility.

Many women are not comfortable listing their financial resources. If that item doesn't come easily to you, don't be concerned. It may not be important, but it's always good to keep in mind where you might go if you need money. Having money can be one of your assets or it can be a resource you may need.

Usually, your resources are hidden in the personal and professional connections you've made over the years.

So whether you need to borrow a car, find a specialty doctor, acquire a loan, or simply crave a new hairdresser, you have access to resources because of your connections to people.

I'm not saying to "use" your friends. One reason I've asked you to list your assets is so you can offer them as resources to others.

Maria said that when she realized that we share our assets *and* we ask for help, it inspired her to ask for the help she needed with her career change.

When she finished the first two inventories, Maria emailed me: "JJ, this speaks to me perfectly. It is like having a deep, enlightening, amazing conversation with a best friend or a psychologist and it inspires me to act upon deep-rooted goals. As a result, I have taken the first step toward training for yoga and nutrition."

For most women, asking for help is not easy. Many of us have this unreasonable idea that we *shouldn't* need help so we *can't* ask for it. We all need help at one time or another. We need to cultivate the courage to ask for help when we need it, without embarrassment, knowing that we have a whole set of assets that we can offer when someone calls on us for help. Asking for help becomes easier when you know that you are willing to be the person who helps someone else. I find that's what women do: we share, reach out, and help each other. Our willingness to be there for each other is a tremendous asset and is helpful for the journey.

Christy leveraged her skills in communication (her asset) to write a newsletter for an interior designer. In exchange, the interior designer installed the tile backsplash and bathroom wallpaper in Christy's house. They traded assets and resources to benefit each in their initiatives.

Make a list of people you know and what resources they may have. You may never need their resource, but if you do, ask. You could use the same list you created for Inventory A, and add another column "Resources." Or create a new list specifically for this category. If you happen to have a network on a social media site such as LinkedIn© or FaceBook©, starting there is another option.

Sarah R., the CEO of Simon and Sylvie, told me that one of the resources that gave her energy and ideas and helped her reinvent herself was redeveloping a rundown neighborhood.

"It was a hotbed for art galleries and restaurants," Sarah said. "There was a lot of buzz that started to hum."

Sarah used her network to get a seat on the neighborhood board of trustees. After attending these meetings, she offered her assets by volunteering to be their marketing go-to person, writing grants, and facilitating meetings.

This was an excellent way to use her skills and access the resources of her neighborhood to grow her customer base for a new initiative. Sarah gained satisfaction and internal energy from this project. She called on her immediate network of people and their networks of people to help remarket a formerly run-down neighborhood. She's proud that today that once dilapidated area has been transformed into a hip new area of town replete with beautiful condos— "and that's a result of my contribution," she says. There's proof that assets and resources go together.

I learn best if I can see my inventories charted in one place. Be sure to find the method or format that works best for you.

My Resource Chart (Fig. 3) is briefer and more direct than some of my other inventories. These charts are works in progress. Add as many columns as you need. Include a note about how you know each person, how to contact him/her, and what each person has to offer. Add a column about what asset you could offer in return.

Sometimes what you need—say an estimate on an antique—will be available through your immediate network and sometimes it won't. Once you start asking people you know, it is more likely someone will say, "I don't know of anyone like that, but a friend of mine got an estimate on her mother's diamond ring and maybe she would know someone who does estimates on antiques."

The Working Woman's GPS:
When the Plan to Have It All Has Led You Astray

Contact	Type of Resource
Todd	Excellent headhunter with pulse on job market
Joan	Local president of women's group; possible speaker's platform and connection to many women
Phil	Graphic Designer for brochures/business cards
Angie	Access to start-ups and neat new initiatives in town; take her to lunch and pick her brain for contacts and local initiatives
Sean	Plumber with many connections
Crystal	Social media expert with a wide network and techniques for on-line networking
Jill	Insurance expert who always makes connections and shares resources; has a large network of people
Stacey	Works for the state with access to start-up resources
Heather	Creative mind; event experience; has related contacts
Tiffany	Early Childcare graduate in neighborhood
Stephanie	Virtual assistant
Jennifer	Website expert
Rose	Works at clinic and knows all local doctors

Fig. 3: Sample Inventory B—Resources

And so it goes. When you ask for help, help seems to arrive in some form or fashion. When I was writing this book I was in search of specific resources to assist with the process. I discussed my book project with a handful of people (professional and personal) in my network of connections, hoping they could guide me to people in their own network. I needed help, and I asked for it. My network of resources came through, connecting me to numerous people all over the United States, whom I've never met. They have given me valuable insights and inspiration on the book-writing process. And all because someone on my resource list knew—or someone they recommended knew—someone who had the assets I needed.

Most nights, before I fall asleep, I ask the Universe to use my assets for the greater good and show me the way to my true calling.

Ask for what you need and desire. You don't have to use my word for the mysterious. You might substitute God, Jehovah, Mohammed, Buddha, Spirit, or Force. You might ask your soul, your inner guide, or your intuition. The name you call whoever or whatever you ask doesn't matter as much as your desire to offer your assets and to request resources to aid you in your journey.

Sometimes, in the oddest of situations, the exact resource I need is unexpectedly brought to me. I could be waiting in line at a store or someone could be sitting next to me on an airplane; it could be someone I meet for the first time at an event. If you ask, knowing that you are willing to share your assets as resources to others, you will receive.

The Working Woman's GPS:
When the Plan to Have It All Has Led You Astray

A few weeks ago, I needed help starting a blog for this book. It seems as though many people are blogging now, but I didn't know anyone who had actually set up their own blogging site. I started asking my network and a few recommendations began trickling back.

A few days later, a friend asked me to help a friend of hers get acquainted in an area in which I had assets and resources. When I looked this new person up on LinkedIn©, guess what? Her hobby was blogging. She was my resource and I became hers.

As you engage in this inventory, you will (1) build your lists of assets and resources, (2) make a list of a few resources you need most immediately, (3) start talking about the resources you need with people in your network, and (4) document how long it takes to connect to the help you need.

Crickett, who had worked early in her marriage, was able to stay home for seven years with her two daughters because of a change in her husband's work situation.

"Those seven years are some of the most wonderful years of my life," Crickett told me. "I was very active with Planned Parenthood® and I joined their board. I was very active at my children's school and I joined their board. I did a lot of volunteer work, and I know that sounds namby-pamby, but the volunteer work really honed my skills for my next career, which was public relations."

Crickett used her natural interests to remain active in her community. One of Crickett's volunteer jobs in the late '80s was at a hospital. When the hospital's ad agency offered her a job, Crickett told them that she didn't have the skills they needed.

"I told them I couldn't write and I didn't know how to use a computer. I had absolutely no classic training in public relations."

But the hospital's hiring manager admired Crickett's work in her volunteer roles and hired her.

"I took the job at $25 an hour," Crickett explained, "and I thought this was a lot of money. I worked part-time for three years and I was promoted to director of new business at this ad agency." Crickett worked until 3 p.m. so she could be home when her daughters came home from school.

This is a wonderful example of how our assets as a person can sometimes outweigh skills gained from formal training. Skills can be learned.

Listing your assets (what you have to give) and the resources (what you can access) can lead to magical connections and stimulate creative pursuits that help you inch closer to the life you really want.

We live in a give-and-take world, or better yet a share-and-share world. When you ask from others, be prepared to be asked to do something for someone else at some point in the future. Always be open to your chance to contribute. Ask for what you need.

This inventory teaches us about two critical pieces necessary to untangle life's threads and calm those inner, shouting voices: We do have resources available, and we do indeed have assets to offer the world.

CHAPTER 8:

Inventory C–
Feelings, Commitments, Risks

That which we understand, we can't blame.
~**Johann Wolfgang von Goethe**

I can imagine that some of you are eager to move on: *Enough of inventories already,* you might be thinking.

Patience is not one of my strong traits either, but this work we're doing requires patience and fortitude. Try not to hurry through. If you must skip ahead, promise yourself you'll return soon. You'll find some great nuggets of questions and explorations that will produce the knowledge you'll need for the journey. If you do skip the work in these last three chapters (and their inventories), you'll likely find, as I did, that you'll have to do them later anyway. Give yourself permission to take the time to do these inventories now, with attention and curiosity. They will benefit your journey sooner rather than later because you'll have a clearer understanding of all that's at stake.

For this inventory, I've grouped three focus areas together because they frequently intertwine. Feelings, commitments, and risks have the equal ability to create in us extreme joy and enthusiasm as well as intense fear and insecurity. Each one, in its own way, is tempestuous, and therefore has something important to teach us.

How Do You Feel?

Feelings are immediate reactions to information. How often do you ask yourself what you're feeling at any given moment? Pay attention to how your feelings change as you move through your days. Being aware of your feelings is essential to making decisions and choices.

Feelings are sometimes intangible: the feeling you get when you make something; the excitement you feel when you are going to see a play or stay home and watch a video; or the special feeling that comes over you when you get home early to spend extra time with your kids. The thrill of achieving a long–held dream, such as going back to school, starting your own business, or turning a beloved hobby into a business is priceless.

As women, we have a deep capacity for feeling. Our ability in this area often makes us good friends, good employees, and good leaders. We often have assets that enable us to easily relate to others.

As working women, some of us are outspoken while others are not. I know many women who have a spectacular gift for empathy and relate well to people in difficult situations.

Feelings will often, and unconsciously, drive many of our decisions, which is why we need to bring our feelings into our awareness. If we are angry at our boss, some of us find a way to begin a nearly imperceptible work slow down. If we feel overwhelming love for our husband or partner, don't we find some lovely surprise to present? If we have a terrible day at work, aren't we often more emotionally unavailable for our families when we come home?

While we are always feeling, we often repress our true feelings. I've done this myself and I find that women I speak with do it as well. Now that I am more aware, I've caught myself responding to the common question, "How are you?" with "Oh, fine." In reality, sometimes I'm not fine.

Take a moment right now to ask yourself how you are feeling. Watch what you do. Do you sigh, become teary, or smile a secret smile? Do you frown and insist you don't know how you feel, and besides, does it matter?

Well, yes, it does matter—very much. Checking your feeling barometer is just as important as checking your bank account or the people, energy, resources, and assets in your life. In fact, feelings may be the most important piece to this inventory. Identifying how you feel requires you to really connect with your inner voice, to check on your emotional health. Being honest with yourself about how you feel doesn't mean you act on those feelings—it means you acknowledge them by writing them down. Look at them. Own them as yours. Don't judge them or yourself. Being honest is the only way you can recognize how your feelings impact your decisions, reactions, and well-being.

This inventory differs from Inventory A because it is not related strictly to the people in your life. It relates to how you feel when you take a walk, lie down for a nap, make an important presentation before a large audience at work, take your children to the park, go on a date, and converse with your boss or co-workers.

To complete this inventory, you have to become aware of your interior climate. Is it sunny and cloudless? Stormy with lightning? Peaceful as a lake on a summer's morning? Chilly and rainy?

When we become aware, we will slow down and notice. Check in with yourself; make a quick note of your inner feelings. You may find it a revealing exercise. Write your feelings down in a small notebook as you go through the day or make mental notes and jot them down at the end of the day. You can even write them with lipstick on your bedroom mirror or in the sandbox with your children. I like to check my feeling barometer several times a day.

Most women I know are so busy working through daily demands and frantically trying to keep all their threads untangled that they don't take time to ask themselves these kinds of loaded questions: "How do I feel, now. Right now? Am I connecting? Uncomfortable? Angry? Rushed? Frantic? Calm? Peaceful? Worried?" Even when we know such inner exploration is good to do, we get forgetful in our busyness or, we just don't take the time. Instead, we're likely to keep on keeping on right into the next thing and the next, in a sort of semi-numb state that gets us through to whatever task or obligation looms. Is this whole-hearted living? As I review my commitments and associated tasks I now ask myself the questions Cynthia Klug[5] asked me in a coaching session:

---

5   *www.positivedgellc.com*

- What do you look forward to doing?
- What makes you smile and gives you energy while you are doing it?
- What do you look forward to doing again?

It's also important to look at what is draining you, what leaves you exhausted, detached, or praying for deliverance. It's just as important to find ways to minimize the negative as it is to accentuate the positive. Feelings are neither good nor bad, but their effect on our physical, emotional, and psychological states are important to consider.

My detailed inventory on feelings might look like this on a given a day (Fig. 4). In the last two inventories, we categorized people and their energies(Inventory A)and assets and resources (Inventory B). Use the same symbols in this assessment:

- (+) Means I feel good and experience positive energy (love, like, am comfortable) from this activity, person, event, or situation
- (-) Means I feel extreme dislike. I feel uncomfortable and do not experience positive energy from this activity, person, event, or situation
- (/) Means I have mixed feelings about this activity, person, event, or situation.

Time	Activity	Details	Energy
6:00 AM	Wake-up call	I love my sleep but need to get my energy flowing	-
7:00	Energy	I always feel better when exercise is a priority	+
7:01	Answer some emails, & make breakfast	Could use some help with all the odds and ends	-
7:25	Get kids up & get their things together	Work to make this quality time	+
8:00	Everyone piles in the car; spend time talking to the kids	Usually fun and a creates a good energy	+
8:30	First call - took the lead, with a customer commitment	Enjoy pushing things forward	+
9:00	Reports due; staff meeting	Administration is needed but not a favorite of mine	-
9:30	1:1 with staff	Work to keep the team focused & motivated	+
10:00	Give presentation	Enjoy knowledge sharing and public speaking	+
12:00	Lunch with business partner	Networking gives me energy	+
1:15	Received urgent data request for a customer meeting	Have to be flexible, helpful, and efficient - stay positive	/
2:00	Call from home, water not working	Mundane – I need help with these house-related chores.	-
4:40	Call from family about dinner	Need to review daily priorities to be sure the key items are completed	/
6:00	Rush to store to get something for dinner; can't have cereal again	Thinking about finding way to make week of meals on Sunday or find help with this	-
6:30	Cook with kids, spill sauce	I love their desire to help but it often creates extra work	/
7:00	Homework	Work to find ways to make it fun	/
8:00	Dishes, laundry, clean kitchen	Need to be sure we have a fresh start in the AM	-
9:30	Back on the PC	Usually exhausted, yet this needs to get done.	/

Fig. 4: Sample Inventory of Daily Feelings (2003)

74

Inventory C–Feelings, Commitments, Risks

> *SUMMARY: What I assessed from this chart is that I need to get help with the demands of the house and the preparation of meals so that I can spend more quality time with my family and allow some time for me later in the day.*

Create a daily feeling inventory for at least a week and capture what you can. I know it won't be perfect because if you're like me, you juggle many things. Make mental notes if you don't have time to log feelings in real time. Later, when you're paying bills or writing a note, jot down what you recall of your feelings during the day and what precipitated them. If you continue noticing your feelings for a few weeks, you will have more information with which to grow. Especially pay attention to strong feelings such as fear and anger or sudden happiness or peace. Notice when you feel *blah*. This inventory should reacquaint you with yourself—and the common feeling themes of your daily life. For inspiration about becoming aware, I recommend Eckhart Tolle's *The Power of NOW.*[6]

---

6   *Eckhart Tolle, The Power of NOW: A Guide to Spiritual Enlightenment (USA: New World Library, 1999; London: Hodder and Stoughton, Ltd., 2001).*

The Working Woman's GPS:
When the Plan to Have It All Has Led You Astray

A monthly assessment on feelings might look like this(Fig. 5):

Activity	Details	Energy
Dinner with Husband	I look forward to a night out.	+
Board Meeting (1)	Believe in the cause; not well-organized & not a great use of my time	-
Work Dinner	Entertaining clients; enjoy the conversations and ability to add value to their business initiatives outside the conference room	+
Soccer Game	Enjoyed watching the kids; make a point to leave my Blackberry in car	+
Travel for fun	Travel with husband and kids; I often take on too much and forget to relax Need to give myself permission to have fun	/
Alone time	Write, workout, enjoy coffee in the park (rare treat); glad to give myself a time of space and renewal	+
Team meeting	Off-site meeting, people disengage	/
Cooking	For me, cooking is only fun when you have the time with no distractions--which never happens in my world	-
House	Bills, clean-up, maintenance, which constantly hangs over my head as an ongoing task.	-
Neighborhood event	Kids loved it; I have great neighbors	+
Board Meeting(2)	Enjoy the cause; find time well-spent; looking to get more involved	+

Fig. 5: Sample Inventory of Monthly Feelings (2003)

> *SUMMARY: When I used this exercise, I realized that I needed to change positions at work; everything related to my work on my list was negative. I also realized that I needed to step down from a board that demanded and deserved more attention than I was able to give. Looking at my daily log, I realized I could make some tweaks in my day that would add more positive energy and remove many of the (-) signs in my columns. Until I did this inventory and saw it on paper, I hadn't realized that a particular situation or person was not aligning with my inner being. Once I had a visual, I worked for months on ways to get more pluses (+) than minuses (-). This inventory had a critical impact on my journey.*

When you recognize how you spend your time and what type of energy it creates, you have a powerful tool at your disposal, especially when you want more from your life but don't know how to make it happen. Look at all your (-) signs; see what you can outsource, barter, or release. Of course you won't be able to remove all of your minus signs at once, but if you can remove a few at a time, it will give you room for more + (positive) signs. To effectively replace the minuses with pluses, you will have to alter a choice, invest in some helping hands, or change your attitude.

These are not easy "asks" of yourself, but you are the only one who can change the direction of your life. Do it one day at a time. Each day is created by the choices you make and how you spend that day. Now, knowing what gives you positive energy, tweak your day. Just one day, even if it's only one hour of one day.

Holly is a thirty-eight-year-old hair stylist and make-up artist. She is married, and they have chosen not to have children. During a verbal inventory I did with her, Holly realized that she's a perfectionist and focused when she cuts hair, but in life outside her work, she tends to be aloof, allowing things to "roll as they may." That's good information—she can do something with it if she is so led.

During her verbal inventory, Holly came up with this insight: "I haven't really done as much as I wanted to do. I think I was afraid of being alone," she said. "I thought I would move and have a big fat career in New York or somewhere. I was always dependent on someone in my life and that kept me here."

Information is power. When you take the time to know how you feel during your day—as it unfolds—and how your feelings change, you'll be more aware of what empowers you, giving you energy, and what holds you back, depleting your energy.

What About Those Commitments?

Commitment includes zeal, devotion, and fidelity. It is an undertaking, a promise, and an obligation. We inventory our commitments to understand where we spend our time. We do this inventory to learn what is too much, where we need help, and what we may need to let go. We may find that some of our commitments are like cement slippers, keeping us stuck.

You may have a personal or professional debt commitment, school expenditures, a house you cannot sell, or a loved one who needs you to be physically close. These commitments affect your life's journey. This is the time to list these commitments, to put them down on paper. List the amount of time you dedicate to each commitment each week.

One of Crickett's commitments is fighting to better women's situations in corporate America, to champion the cause of working women.

"I fought for us," she says. "What that means to me," Crickett explained, "is recognition of the disparity in the world. And, you can quantify it. . . six ways to Sunday with wage scale and everything. You just have to look around the board rooms, often times the people seated all look the same. . . . But it's getting so much better."

As a single mom, Cathy had an interesting way of handling her commitments to her children. She told them to "give permission to yourself to be exceptional. I said that to both of my kids when they were eight and nine, Cathy said. 'I don't care what sport or extracurricular project you pick. But I want you to pick one you're passionate about, that you want to be exceptional in. Not excellent. Exceptional. I will move every single mountain for you to achieve.' They each picked something, and so we have their goals that we share. I have my business goals and my business side. Then we have our family goals. Then we have each of their passionate goals. And I think that, if that's how you structure your life, if everybody has a passion, all three of us have a passion. We all do everything to support the others. In that way, you create this bond where nobody feels guilty. Everybody feels empowered and they are participating and helping and collaborating to make everybody a success."

Your commitment inventory could look like this one (Fig. 6) from a friend of mine:

Commitment	Details	Hours/Wk
Family	Love, attention, maintenance, cook, clean	49
Aunt	Care for her 3 days/week, laundry and doctor appts	13
Family Med Issues	Medical condition that requires weekly appts.	5
School	Work 1/2 day, 2 days a week, to help with tuition	7
Animals	2 dogs that need exercise and attention	7
Board	One board seat with bi-monthly meetings	1
Group	Women's Group – organize, lead, and manage	2
Job	Part-time job	25

Fig. 6: Friend's Commitment Inventory

Thirty-nine-year-old Leslie is an entrepreneur who has fostered her own company. She has chosen not to have children.

"Do you struggle with time commitments?" I asked her.

"For sure," Leslie said. "Staying married takes a certain amount of effort and attention as does keeping up with friendships and family relationships. I have nieces and nephews, so I've committed to being a favorite aunt. That takes work, but it's hardly work."

Kimberly described herself as the more focused of all her women friends. "When I have things to do, I am very disciplined," she said. "Senior year of college I was focused on landing a job and getting high grades, and I had to make some sacrifices socially. My friends still joke about it: They say I came out of the womb with a suit on and a resume in hand."

Now out of the boys' clubs in the financial industry, Kimberly works in medical sales in Chicago. She has made some challenging commitments. "Sometimes I get spread way too thin," she admitted. "I have always been involved in many activities outside of work, and I know when I commit to being involved, I really put my all into it. I'm not just checking a box to say *I've done it.*" She's learned that her most satisfying connections are with people who work very hard to honor their commitments, like she does.

Cathy spent twenty-two years as a global merger acquisitions lawyer, traveling around the world, making huge financial deals. Her last deal, she told me, was a $4.7 billion investiture. Then she realized something.

The Working Woman's GPS:
When the Plan to Have It All Has Led You Astray

"The business of law, the business of accounting, and the business of other professions became, for me, a commodity," Cathy said. "It wasn't about relationship anymore. It was about the cheapest price, the quickest turn around. It wasn't a profession anymore. . . . When you take a look at who you are as a person, and your values, and what you believe in, sometimes the professional path you got on doesn't match with who you are. If you don't end your commitment to that path, you become terribly, terribly unhappy."

Cathy offers a method of measurement. Who are you as a person? What are your values? What do you believe in?

I offer another: What doesn't match that which your inner self is asking you to do? What is the best use of your time now?

What's Your Appetite for Risk?

A risk is a chance, a gamble. Risks are the dragons life asks us to tame.

When we take a risk, we come face to face with fear; we have no certainty about the final result and we can never be sure of the outcome. Some people feel most alive when they are risking their fortunes or their lives. Marriage is a risk, but so are most major decisions.

Not all journeys require big risks, but even the most ordinary journey requires many critical decisions that could be considered risky. When I decided to leave Georgia for Ohio to get married, I didn't initially see this decision as a risk. However, looking back, I see that my decision led to several other major decisions that led to risk taking. I had no idea how any of my decisions or risks would turn out. I took a risk on a relationship I thought was my life partner. In making that decision and moving, I took a big risk with my career trajectory, and I risked all the associated networks of people I had established. Back in early 2000, LinkedIn© wasn't yet an idea.

At the time, I felt confident that I could undo any choice I made as easily as I had made it. Knowing what I know now, that isn't always the case. Ignorance is bliss, and necessary, I suppose, since we probably won't ever know for certain how a choice—which can be considered a risk—will turn out. Even with this unknown element lurking, it's important to make choices, take calculated risks, and press forward. Even if our choices don't turn out as we expect, there is often a hidden gift especially meant for us.

What's your appetite for risk?

In comments posted to a question I raised on my blog about "What We Learn from Risk", the following responses are representative of those I received on February 22, 2011:

- "I learned that I have the capacity to bounce."
- "I learned that I had more courage than I thought"
- "I learned confidence."
- "I learned everything about myself."
- "I learned strength within."

Holly and her husband are interested in living by a body of water, but she admits that taking risks scare them so they have not yet made the decision.

"We just have to stop being afraid," Holly said. "We keep waiting for each other to do it—whether it is as simple as a family trip or a life-changing decision such as relocation. I'm waiting for him to make the decision and he's waiting for me to make it. He doesn't want to make the wrong decision because then it will be his fault. I'm too much of a chicken. We just sort of laugh and say that nothing will get done."

Right before Paulette became an officer in her company, the company made a change that required management to contribute toward their health care for the first time, but the union workers were exempted from contributing toward health care. Paulette believed she had to speak up. She knew that speaking up in the face of a corporate policy with which she disagreed was a risk, but it was one she had to take.

At one of her first senior management meetings, the CEO opened the floor to questions, and Paulette raised her hand.

"I stood up and shared that there was a tremendous amount of negative backlash from this decision. I asked my question about fairness: why one group had to pay and the other didn't. I said that the decision was not made in concert with each other... why management had to pay partial health care yet the union workers did not. I remember my boss telling me after that meeting 'that was very brave of you... stupid, but very brave.' I could not *not* say something."

"Did you get any negative backlash for speaking your mind?" I asked her.

"I did not," she said. "If something is being said that you don't agree with, you need to speak up. That's one of several things I will tell a new group of people when I come into an organization or when someone new comes into my organization. If you don't agree with what is going on and you say nothing, you are essentially agreeing with that with which you disagree. You have a responsibility for mutual success if you disagree."

But risk taking is only as valid as the commitment you make to it. Paulette explained her commitment. "I was very, very watchful of how the women in my organization functioned. It bothered me tremendously if I ever saw them defer to the male counterparts. I worked on that. I had a diversity committee. I participated on it and that committee included members at all levels of my organization. There were only about twenty of us. But we worked on that issue. It drove me crazy when women deferred."

If you are already overcommitted, there is likely little room for taking risks. For example, if you're a mother of young children and/or the primary caregiver of an elderly person, then taking on another major commitment will likely require you to call on a few more hands (resources) to help you before you take a risk that entails a large commitment of time.

Cathy—who began as a global acquisitions lawyer, became an Episcopal priest, and then began her own green company—had some strong feelings on the subject of risk.

"I don't think young women do enough taking of risk," Cathy said. "And in large part, that's because women are more risk averse. We have to constantly challenge ourselves, particularly young women, about being willing to take risks. And that's whether it's starting a business or going for broke on given projects. It's daring to step out and speak up when you have a wave of brilliance. I think young women particularly need to step out. And it makes a remarkable difference if they can take risks wherever they are instead of being a participant. Be a leader. Women are great leaders. They are fabulous leaders. But they're just reticent, naturally reticent."

First, list the risks you've already taken, then note the risks you only *thought* about taking. Reflect on your appetite for risk; the answers are important for you and the people around you.

Here are some starter questions:

- What dreams have you accomplished and how did risk—even a small one—come into play?
- What are the potential risks of staying in your exact situation?
- Are there future choices that are risky, yet just the thought of them energizes you?
- How will these future choices and their related risks advance your goals?
- Who else may need to be involved to ensure the success of such choices?
- What dream seems no longer possible? Why? What would you be risking?

Often, risk requires a certain sacrifice of existing choices to move forward.

Shelley is facing just such risk—and its underbelly of sacrifice. You may remember that Shelley, mom of two girls, found a problem with the Plan in all the "stuff" there was to do to have it All. She works as a contractor for a software company while holding and trying to keep many threads untangled that represent all her choices around family, home, and extras.

Shelley did an inventory "to get out of the rat race," she said.

"Every day I think about what could change," she said. "The reality is I wish my husband made the income I make and I made his. Then it would be a much easier decision. It's hard for me to walk away from my job, and then I know the pressure is really on him to maintain everything for our family."

"Would you work if you didn't need the money?" I asked Shelley.

"In a limited capacity, probably part-time," Shelley confided. "I couldn't *not* work, but I would want to work in something more fulfilling, something that would make me happy."

Sacrifice can mean many different things. Sarah R. worked for a year at a job she "absolutely hated" because she needed to pay the bills. "I call it my 'year of patience,' Sarah said. "I proved to myself I could do it. Right now, I'm looking for the right job, not just a job that will provide a paycheck."

The dragon of risk comes out of its cave every so often and asks us to identify opportunities or to make adjustments to our existing choices that are likely to require some level of risk. No matter how comfortable we might be, life will find ways to challenge us, on behalf of our growth.

What is life asking of you? Could you be on the verge of a life-changing risk? If so, you may be getting ready to accelerate in a new direction.

CHAPTER 9

Inventory D–Dreams & Desires

Despite my thirty years of research into the feminine soul, I have not been able to answer . . . the great question that has never been answered: what does a woman want? ~**Sigmund Freud**

Do You Let Yourself Dream?

When you leave this earth, what do you hope you will have accomplished? How do you want to be remembered? How many lives will you have touched? What will you have fostered, built, created, or concluded? What would not have happened had you not been here, on earth, in your body?

These questions were the impetus for this book.

As I moved through my thirties and approached my forties, I hired career coaches to facilitate some of my thoughts and desires into plans. I came across some wonderful coaches but found the greatest synergy with Cynthia M. Klug. She was poised, purposeful, and effective. During our second session, she assigned homework. My first thoughts were anything but eager: "Ridiculous! I can hardly complete the tasks I already have! To add these exercises to the list would be impossible."

The Working Woman's GPS:
When the Plan to Have It All Has Led You Astray

Then one night, while everyone in my house was asleep, I began working on an upcoming presentation for work. Despite my decision not to follow through on Cynthia's assignment, it kept nagging at me. Finally, I opened a new document on my computer and began to write. I read it over once, saved, and closed it.

When I next met with Cynthia, I opened the document on my PC, and read it aloud to her. "If I could be so lucky," I thought as I read with tears rolling down my cheeks. Cynthia's exercise had ignited a passion in me that felt familiar, but I hadn't really acknowledged it or allowed myself to do something about it. Deep down, I really wanted to make the impact in the world that I had written about in the wee hours of the night.

The assignment Cynthia gave me had two parts. Part One was to "describe your seventieth birthday party." I'll share part of what I wrote that night.

First of all, I decided I had to have a setting for the party. Without thinking much about it, I wrote:

"an Elegant Event with friends and family
from various locations. The food is fabulous
with some of the best chefs around. The
ocean air is refreshing while laughter fills the
room."

Then I really began typing:

"Many people who have traveled the world
with us comment on fond memories of food,
wine, and amazing locations. I enjoy the
good will of friends, co-workers, and families
I've influenced. Close friends comment on

my impact on women, the success of my
children, my many years of mentoring, my
years of contributing to nonprofits, my
natural ability to bring people together,
my deep love for my husband, friends, and
family, my addiction to work, my vivacity,
and my desire to do more (unbridled
ambition).

Part Two of Cynthia's assignment was, "What is your
bio at seventy years old?"

Here's what I wrote, in part:
"JJ has lived a life of passion and
inspiration. JJ has been able to successfully
build a sensational career while creating
a venue that provides women with a
supportive and inspirational voice.
Throughout the years, her profits were
well distributed among local, national, and
global charities to empower women in all
aspects of life."

When I read it to Cynthia, I felt my true passion burst
in me; my calling was evident. What I wrote that memorable night came from a place well beyond my mind. As
I said, I wrote this in the wee hours when little feet were
resting in bed, after the dryer had stopped running, and at
a time when my mind was not occupied with the comings
and goings of everyday life.

I can't say I thought about what to write; rather I
started writing. I just started typing and let whatever was
meant to appear on the page appear. I was a conduit. I

know some of it sounds far-fetched, but that's okay. Our wants may not manifest in reality, but our dreams and desires are individual and special—and meant for us.

The deep connection that occurred within me when I fully grasped the words I had written was the beginning of the late nights during which much of the material for this book was documented. I probably would have written something eventually—but never this early in my life and not likely with the passion I feel about the Plan that has been the relevant operating system for women for too long.

So now, I'm going to ask you to do what Cynthia asked of me.

Find a quiet place during a quiet time and let your mind wander. Let yourself "Describe your 70th birthday party." Then write your bio at age seventy.

See what appears on the page or in a notebook. Be truthful and take nothing into consideration other than what you dream about and desire for your life. It doesn't matter what your present financial situation is or whether you have the resources to accomplish your dream. It doesn't matter if you don't have time right now for what you really want to do. All that matters is that you list your dreams and desires—without worrying about obstacles.

During the interviews, I found that women, especially as they near forty, begin to think about a larger life purpose.

Christy mentioned this when we talked.

"Ironically, I'm going to church more in the last six months than I ever did. But going to church isn't the religious spiritualism I'm talking about. It's more about find-ing the inner harmony where you make yourself happy. There's calmness to my life that I didn't have before."

Leslie feels the difference too. "I'm in the middle of making a commitment to being a pioneer in my own life," she said. "Ignoring the well-worn ruts and roads that ev-eryone is on, stopping the parade and making up my own structures, goals, paths, my own road, my own categories, or buckets. And then, just putting it out there. So it feels wrong to say I'm happy. But to say I'm happy would be the 'right answer.' I would say I am lucky. I'm lucky that we live in the United States, that I'm a woman. We don't have to worry about genocide. We have a lot of freedom and choices. I'm right in the middle of making more of those choices consciously; that makes sense for me."

What do you dream about? Find time to let your mind and heart wander.

If it were not for this particular inventory, I wouldn't have fully realized at this point in my life my desire to cre-ate an initiative that encouraged, empowered, and elevated women. The desire had been inside me for years, and I was already working in small ways toward this goal, but it wasn't realized until I made *me* a priority, hired a coach, and then became focused in my efforts. That exercise was one of the catalysts for this initiative. Thank you, Cynthia, for suggesting that I change my lens and view my life from a different perspective.

When you do these two assignments with your most honest and connected self, be prepared to catch a glimpse of what's calling you.

PART III:
REVISING THE COURSE, BUILDING CONFIDENCE

CHAPTER 10

Start Simple, Easy Does It

The journey of a thousand miles begins with a single step.
~Confucius

To reach the life that beckons us, it's up to us. I am the only person who can take the first step toward change on my own behalf, and so, too, are you.

Most women I know have enjoyed at least some of the many benefits promised by the Plan to have it All. Yet we have also found that the Plan, predefined and one-size-fits-all, has left many of us overworked, overcommitted, and unfulfilled. In the process of trying to have it All, we lost part of ourselves.

Now is the time to take a first step—any small step will do—toward a life of purpose, inspiration, and fulfillment. If you've worked on the inventories, you should have at least an inkling of where you yearn to be. You've caught glimpses of what inspires you and what stirs the truest part of your *self*. In this section, I suggest some small, concrete changes that will help generate the momentum to change course a little or to risk a leap into a self-designed Plan of your own choosing—a Plan that is not driven by society's Plan, our culture, or other women's plans.

The Working Woman's GPS:
When the Plan to Have It All Has Led You Astray

When I reached this step on my journey, I found that there were many small, relatively easy changes I could put into practice in just minutes. These small changes repositioned me in a slightly new and revised direction. Some of the changes were as simple as choosing not to do one thing and choosing to do another. In some cases, I worked to remove a self-deprecating attitude that had become a problem. With each step, each small change, I felt a renewed energy and determination that the life I expected *was* possible.

As you shift your perspective, stride with more confidence, and make the small adjustments I'm recommending, my hope is that you will find your genuine energy sources. We cannot do everything at once; rather, we start small and build on each step, which will further empower us to move forward.

As you become more determined, your determination will create an inner perseverance that bubbles up within you to find the path that creates energy and purpose within you. A new sense of possibility begins to take shape. Your inner voice is no longer shouting at you; it is becoming softer and gentler because you are paying attention to it. Those tangled threads that used to drive you crazy become easier to untangle. You feel more peaceful, grounded, and centered.

If you already feel fulfilled in your work life and have succeeded in creating a life of purpose and inspiration, I congratulate you! Still, I encourage you to explore your feelings and to include a variety of the suggestions in this section in your own life. There are always growth edges out there, chances to grow ever deeper and more peaceful. Life always calls us to explore the hard questions. What next? What needs less? What needs more?

I suggest we begin by acknowledging this truth: Most of the time, people do the very best they can. As women, we tend to be terribly self-critical. We blame ourselves because we don't think our best is good enough. We forget that no one is perfect. Yet how many women are prone to thinking they are somehow exempt, that they *should* be a little better. We tend to think we can sleep less, eat less, and work more without grave consequences—a loss of ourselves, our passion, our sources of inspiration.

Leslie had something to say about expectations: "That idea of having it all and having everything work all at the same time is really restrictive and unrealistic. It's impractical. It's frustrating that you can see certain areas humming at a good clip at certain times, but it's crazy to expect it will *all* go well at the same time."

Take that first step. Release unreasonable expectations and acknowledge you are doing the best you can. Don't be so hard on yourself or others. Include a little self-care in every day. Be purposeful in your intentions. Intend to do no harm, and remember to do no harm to yourself as well as to others.

Let's give up guilt and self-judgment. Guilt is a pretty useless way to focus energy. Let's agree that we are all imperfect. Let's give ourselves some gentle love and compassion, even when we make mistakes.

Step 1: Cherish your perfect and imperfect self.

CHAPTER 11

Jumpstart Your Day

Welcome every morning with a smile. Look on the new day as another special gift from your creator, another golden opportunity to complete what you were unable to finish yesterday. ~**Og Mandino**

When I lost my way, I had to force myself to get out of bed in the morning. Even though I realized that being late to work would turn my day upside down, it didn't seem to faze me.

Morning Mirror: Who Is Looking Back at You?

Some days I desperately wanted to go anywhere else than to the meetings and commitments I had scheduled— somewhere more important and productive where I could contribute more solutions to more interesting problems. I kept hitting the snooze button; I didn't have the energy to get out of bed, let alone leap out of bed, glad to be alive.

Once I did stumble out of bed, I had trouble mustering the energy to pull together a coordinated outfit and wash and style my hair. When I looked in the mirror, I hardly recognized the person staring back at me. Who was she? And where had all her passion and energy gone? Where was the go-getter I once knew? Where was the person who had energy to spare? Staring back at me was a woman who didn't have the energy, the passion, or the momentum to live her best life.

It took me some time to realize that starting my day like this was *not* going to catapult me to a life of inspiration. I had to work on myself and evaluate the life I had created through my choices. How could I turn my life and my mornings around?

Whether or not you're a 'morning' person, morning energy is a great predictor of how the day is apt to go. A strong energy pulse in the morning is likely to predict a wonderfully engaging day. You wake up glad to be alive, grateful that you are in the world, that you have people you love deeply, including yourself. You have a job that fulfills you, and you are contributing to this world in some way that also fulfills you. Strong pulse people often start the day alone, with a few moments to themselves because they understand that taking care of themselves helps them care for their families and their work; they have energy that lasts all day.

Weak pulse people might need some emergency interventions! By waking up with a weak pulse, you awake exhausted, bored, without energy, and often complaining. You never wake thinking, "I appreciate being alive today." You're unmotivated and sluggish from the get-go; it's unlikely that you eat a healthy breakfast or have a regular exercise schedule. You may feel that you're missing something from your life, fantasizing that if you found that someone or something you might change and become

happy. We already have what we need; that needing
something or someone else is a lie we tell ourselves. The
truth is: We have everything we need to rescue ourselves.

If you know your morning energy level, you can use
that information to take your morning energy pulse,
thereby gaining some understanding of whether you are
temporarily stuck or moving along well on your journey.
Knowledge is power.

- What gets you out of bed? (you, the alarm, your
  partner, kids, work, job, pet)
- How do you feel when you get going in the
  morning? (exhilarated, excited, exhausted,
  discouraged, worried)
- What parts of your day excite you? (every part,
  only when I get home, only when I fall into bed,
  nothing about the day excites me)
- When was the last time you were excited to start
  the day? (this morning, last week, last year, can't
  remember)

If you have a weak energy pulse, it's important to find
one or more sources that provide the energy you need to
start your day on a positive, uplifting note. Doing so will
change your day, I promise. Below are a few suggestions.
Try at least one, even if you don't feel like it:

- Spend some time alone in silence or create
  positive conversation with the people around you;
- Start your day with something you enjoy;
- Get your heart pumping with fifteen minutes
  doing yoga, jumping jacks, walking, or bike
  riding;

- Contribute something positive to online groups;
- Read something you want to learn more about; and
- Eat a good breakfast.

Cathy has a strong morning routine. "I get up about 5:30 a.m., and take a six o'clock run. I run five miles a day," she said. "I am just passionate about my yard and sports. So I do those things that bring me joy in small ways. But usually I do them outside the hours that my kids see me. Because when I'm home, I'm theirs."

Do You Spend a Little Time with Yourself?

I've learned that starting the morning on *my* time rather than waiting for the kids to get up or my alarm to go off has helped me gain control of my day from its first moment.

At a conference a few months ago, I met Suzanne, a terrific, high-powered working woman and mother of triplets. Suzanne shared with me that although she loved her sleep, she *really* loved to spend the first few minutes of her day with a hot cup of coffee in her kitchen by herself, before anyone else woke up. It meant she had to get up at 5 a.m., but she called it her time to "just be." Without those thirty minutes of time alone at the start of her day, she could almost guarantee the day would take on a life of its own and out of her control.

I recommend adopting Suzanne's suggestion. That's what I've done. After talking to Suzanne, I found a way to essentially trick myself into getting up a few minutes early to do something for myself. I record my favorite show on the DVR that sits in front of my treadmill—and only on that TV. So if I want to watch the program, I know I have to get on that treadmill.

At first, it was tough to get on the treadmill first thing in the morning, and I even stopped watching the show for a period of time. But I missed the entertainment and energy. Soon I was lacing up my shoes, stepping on that treadmill, enjoying a few minutes of my favorite show, and getting my body revved up and toned.

Now, I'm with Suzanne; I like my morning time to set my own agenda before everyone else tries to get a piece of it. This practice has helped me set my daily compass, determine my priorities, and focus my energy to better handle whatever comes my way.

When the family wakes up, I'm confident, relaxed, and ready. I'm more inclined to respect myself, my time, and my voice throughout the day.

Step 2: Start the day by revving your energy.

CHAPTER 12

Become Contagious

A smile is the light in the window of your face that tells people you're at home. ~**Author Unknown**

As we move through our days, we are often buried in our mental to-do lists, rushing toward the next thing, or planning for the future. As a result, we often have no connection to what is happening right before our eyes. We are often unaware of the people who quickly pass in and out of our lives.

When I was at that in-between stage in my journey, I was often confused and disconnected from myself and the world around me. My life had many wonderful aspects. Although society would've said I had "made it," I had an overwhelming sense of being lost and unfulfilled. When people would ask, "How are you?" I would put on a fake smile and respond, "Fine."

I had lost my own truth, which was evident on my face as I lost my genuine smile.

One of the first conscious choices I made was to smile and make eye contact with each person I saw. I made an intention to be genuine, and I trusted that eventually my genuine smile would return. Within a few days, I saw a distinct difference in myself and the people with whom I interacted.

Several benefits became quickly apparent. I learned that my smile was contagious. I found that the more I shared a genuine smile, the more people reciprocated. The more effort I put into smiling and making eye contact, the more present I became to all aspects of my life.

This small effort yielded big benefits. When people re-Turned my smile, it positively energized me and improved my energy pulse. Don't take my word for it, try it for yourself. Conduct your own little experiment and see if there's a difference in you and in others when you smile. Does smiling, and having it returned, energize you?

You can smile even if you feel poorly in every sense of the word, even if you don't have your basic needs met. You still have within you the energy to share your love for life with another individual through eye contact and a smile. You need only to be in the moment rather than lost in thought about the past or future. A smile can have mutual benefits by putting you in the present moment and by providing others an energy lift.

Check out these quotes and statistics—so much has been documented about the act of smiling:

- Someone once said, "Of all the things you wear, your expression is the most important."[7]
- Christopher Peterson, Ph.D., a professor at the University of Michigan, said, "The research is very clear. There is a link between optimistic attitudes and good health. It has been measured in a variety of ways. Overall, we have found that optimistic

---

7   *Janet Lane, actress*

people are healthier. Their biological makeup is different. They have a more robust immune system." A simple thing like smiling more is a boost to your immune system.[8]

• According to a study published in the November 2004 issue of the *Archives of General Psychiatry*, smiling helps us live longer. Elderly people in the sixty-five to eighty-five age range who were optimistic about good things happening were less likely to die from all causes than the most pessimistic people (who always expected the worst). Even after researchers adjusted the results for age, smoking status, alcohol consumption, physical activity, and other health measures, the optimists were 71 percent less likely to die than the pessimists.[9]

A study by the British Dental Health Foundation reports that a smile gives the same level of stimulation as eating 2,000 chocolate bars; it feels like being in love.[10] A smile is *that* invigorating.

Mother Teresa commented, "Peace begins with a smile." A smile has been called a universal language all over the world. The Zen Buddhist teacher Thich Nhat Hanh said, "Sometimes your joy is the source of your smile, but sometimes your smile can be the source of your joy."[11]

A smile can be an honest spiritual connection with another being, a true connection with people, animals,

8   http://ariselifeskills.wordpress.com/2009/04/22/smile-the-many-bene-fits-of-a-big-grin-brought-to-you-by-arise-life-skills/
9   Ibid.
10   Ibid.
11   Ven. Thich Nhat Hanh http://www.quoteworld.org/quotes/6225

plants, stars, sky, trees, and flowers. Again, use your own term if you don't like "spiritual." I use "spiritual" to mean the core of the soul, the connection that is raw, unbiased, and natural. You may choose force or energy—and those words can certainly apply to the power that a smile can have. Use whatever word sits well and comfortably inside you.

It's difficult to be a fully human and fully spiritual being when we are sad, angry, or disappointed because those negative energies consume most of the space inside us. Smiling purposefully by making a conscious effort will upset those negative energies and exchange them with positive and connected energies. A purposeful smile could be the beginning of something grand.

If you're having trouble generating a smile, do something outrageously silly: jump on the bed; bake cookies; go to the park, settle into a swing seat then swing; jump rope; or play hopscotch. Engage your inner child (which needs silliness and play) to rediscover your genuine smile.

"You have to be happy for yourself," Leah said.

- How many times during your day can you practice connecting with another person through eye contact and a smile?
- Begin smiling with people you know and expand to people you pass as you move through your day.
- Notice how smiling affects your own energy.

If, at first, you find it hard to generate a genuine smile, practice. Smile with the intention of becoming genuine and in no time at all, your "fake" smile will transform itself.

When you run into someone who doesn't return your smile, "Don't worry", says Emma Seppala, Ph.D., "it's only temporary."

Seppala writes, ". . . the sight of another person smiling can activate your zygomatic facial muscles (or 'smile muscles') and make you feel happier. This may be due to what have been called 'mirror neurons' in the brain, which get activated both when we do an action and when we see someone else do that same action. Incidentally, this is a great reason not to feel embarrassed when you smile at someone and he/she doesn't smile back! Chances are, you are activating his micro-muscles, making his/her day better, and he will smile at the next person he meets!"[12]

So we *can* become contagious by smiling. A smile creates positive energy and makes us more beautiful; life becomes more manageable and the world looks brighter.

Initiate your sparkle. Smile on Purpose. See how it works and tell us about it on the blog.

Step 3: Become contagious—smile.

---

12   *Emma Seppala, Ph.D., "Shift Your Body, Change Your Mind," Spirituality & Health, 2010 September/October: 61:58-61.*

CHAPTER 13:

Zoom in on the Positive

The future hasn't happened yet and the past is gone.
So I think the only moment we have is right here and
now, and I try to make the best of those moments, the
moments that I'm in. ~**Annie Lennox**

Would you like to become more positive? It's not as hard as you may think.

When I needed to find some way to develop more positive energy, I started a little notebook to capture positive things I saw, heard, or noticed. Then I could lean on those positive things in my notebook when I needed a burst of energy.

Positive things may happen to you or you may watch them happen to others. The point is that the more you notice the positives in life, the more abundant the positives become.

Nancy, who lives in Florida, called me a few months ago after we had a discussion at an event. She admitted, quite honestly, that it was easier for her to focus on the negative because it was more aligned with how she felt inside. During that initial conversation, I asked her to name five positive things that had happened that week, but her response made it quickly apparent that she thought this would be impossible.

I asked Nancy to commit to buying a small notepad and placing it in her purse. She agreed. Every time she witnessed or experienced a positive interaction or event she promised to document it in her notepad.

After one week, she called me, excited. She shared that she had actually captured ninety-two wonderful experiences in one week. What was even more amazing was the energy in her voice. Nancy was not only able to recognize when an exchange or experience was positive, but noticing it, she was then able to harvest and share some of that positive energy. As a result, her positive energy increased.

Oprah, one of my personal inspirations and heroines, suggests keeping an "Appreciation Log," which is how I initially started this practice. This kind of positive journaling often readjusts our lens on life. We think things are so bad, yet by noticing the positive events that happen or finding things to appreciate, like a cool breeze on a hot day, a favorite song on the radio, a special kiss at the end of a long day, our child's smile, a friend's success, or an unexpected gift of time or good health, we open ourselves to more of the same good stuff.

Here's what you do: Force yourself to find five good things every day and write them down—things you notice, things you experience, good ideas that come, something someone said. Even though some things in your life might be difficult or painful, there are still things that, if you notice them, will make you smile. Be grateful for everything that makes you smile. Remember to appreciate yourself for doing the best you can!

Over the years, as I've been zooming in on more positive things, I've noticed that what I give out comes back to me in kind. I've made a conscious effort to fill myself with good energy and move away from sources that deplete my energy.

As we move through life, we need positive, high-energy, upbeat, and lighthearted people. To attract such people, we need to develop those qualities in ourselves because we know they will be looking to us for positive companionship and guidance.

Gillian seemed to have reached a similar conclusion about negative and positive energy. "When you're exuding positive energy in this world," she said, "you'll get positive energy back. It's all about exchanging energy."

She's right. By changing the lens through which we view our world—from negative to positive—we change our world.

Step 4: Focus on the positive.

CHAPTER 14

Lessons All Around Us

The one lesson I have learned is that there is no substitute for paying attention. ~**Diane Sawyer**

As eager as we may be to move on to a better space in life—and I sure was—I believe it is also true that, right now, we are exactly where we need to be. For our journeys to turn a corner and accelerate, we need to learn the important life lessons from our current situation.

Life is a teacher; we are its pupils. Whenever a challenging situation arises, I ask myself, What am I meant to learn from this?

For example, I've learned, through multiple opportunities, to be patient with myself and others. Over and over, I've been tested in this area through challenging and often frustrating situations. These situations have honed my skills and ensured I was ready to embark on a more complex, important, and fulfilling journey. Learning patience may not be your lesson, but I bet life is testing you in some way, like a teacher, hoping you "get" the lesson.

My patience was continually tested whenever I was engaged in project-based work. I was driven to either initiate the project or complete the project.

The Working Woman's GPS:
When the Plan to Have It All Has Led You Astray

My gung-ho work ethic and take-charge attitude wasn't always what was needed for the ultimate success of the project. Through a series of good and bad situations, and with the help of some great mentors, I had to learn that being a leader means stepping back from the actual work and recognizing and embracing the strengths and talents of other people. It was more important that I learned to encourage, guide, and mentor others to take the leadership role than always taking the lead myself. One of my important life lessons about patience translated from work projects to other situations in my community and at my children's school.

I had to reflect: Yes, I can choose to lead every project inside or outside of my office, but should I? Is this the best use of my time? I learned that if I gave others a chance to lead, and myself a chance to follow, I had energy left to focus on other initiatives.

I have to admit that patience was a tough lesson because it meant that timelines might be extended and outcomes could differ from my expectations. The key word here is "my;" "my" is not always welcome. I wasn't sure I wanted to learn this lesson because it was difficult to step back yet critical to know where and what needed my attention.

A bonus lesson: When I took the time to invest in the people around me, I experienced incredible energy. When I stepped back and let others take the helm, encouraged their talents, and supported them in their leadership roles, I felt empowered in ways I would never have imagined. Without learning this lesson about patience, I could never have achieved many of my other life goals because I thought I needed to do everything I touched. In reality, sometimes I have to follow, and other times I need to sit out the whole project.

My time also became more productive when I let go of some of the daily responsibilities in my home. I found that my time is better used in enabling other women. I now have two wonderful women who are excellent at handling the demands of my house and everyone in it; they often do a much better job than I of keeping everything untangled. It is possible, if you do not have the means, to barter services (think back to your assets and resources) with loved ones, neighbors, and friends. I still do this, too.

I notice women find letting go difficult; it took me years. During this time, life threw me new lessons and increased my awareness so that finally, I was able to let go. Once I learned it, the lesson became invaluable.

Of course, we can always refuse to learn the lessons, and continue to operate in old, familiar ways. What I've discovered is that by trying to get out of a particular situation too soon, without learning the lesson, it's pretty certain that I'll soon find myself circling back and having to deal with a similar situation with a similar lesson. Life always presents us with opportunities to grow.

Life lessons are important. To understand *what* lesson life is asking you to learn and *why*, these questions might help:

- What don't you like about a current situation?
- Why don't you like it?
- What changes do you think will make it better?

- What is the lesson? Have you discovered it?
- What is keeping you from learning the lesson?

Step 5: Appreciate life's teaching moments.

CHAPTER 15

Are You a Practicing Polluter?

Whoever gossips to you will gossip about you.
~**Spanish Proverb**

What if I pulled aside a few of your friends, family, or co-workers and asked them to describe your communication style? Would they say you were up-front and honest? Brutally frank? Timid and mousy? Forthright and clear? Kind and sincere? Would their assessment match the kind of communication you strive for every day? Would they casually mention how often you slip into negativity?

Become aware of what comes out of your mouth, including your tone of voice and the words you use. Your vibe and body language are also important. Each is an expression of *self.*

A next small but critical step is to filter out negativity in whatever form it manifests. You know, the quick spurt of words or conversation that may attack others and undermine them as people or the critical voice in your head that undermines you. Either way, that "voice" needs to be noticed, acknowledged, and minimized.

What's Your Tone?

The people in your life all have their objectives and goals, principles to live by, and political and religious alliances, which may or may not align with your goals, principles, and beliefs. We can disagree with others; the important thing is *how* we do it.

Is your tone dismissive or snide? Does it have an underbelly of envy? Is it patronizing or condescending? Do you feel angry or resentful as you speak? (Those emotions come through.) Is what you say genuine or phony?

Are you unsure of what your tone is? At the pace we move through our scheduled tasks, it's not unusual to miss noticing how our communications are interpreted. Try a little experiment at home: Speak in only a positive way to the people you live with. What happens when you choose not to criticize, complain, whine, gossip, backstab, or yell?

At times, it can be difficult to *not* be negative in a work environment. But it's not impossible to be positive.

I've been in the corporate world for seventeen years, and I make an active effort to remove myself from negative talk. Negativity is poison for me, my co-workers, and the company. If I can't say something positive, I say nothing. Yet I still smile as I walk away, leaving negativity behind. I pull out my BlackBerry and begin reading emails, or drift away in thought. By doing so, I haven't been fired or demoted.

But I haven't always been this way. I have a matter-of-fact communication style; I often call it as I see it. Sometimes that isn't helpful, and it is often unnecessary. At one time, I found it so easy to pull someone down or to disagree with someone's proposed initiative. I was quick to size up people and offer an unkind comment. What I said often hurt or bothered the other person and brought their energy level to zero. I had to ask myself, "What am I doing?" Did I want to help or hinder humankind and the world?

We all need to actively mute the negative in both our internal and external conversations. If you're not sure if you need to mute the negative, try a quick Self-Communication Audit. I do one regularly. It helps me notice and keep track of what I say in each and every interaction. The audit has three steps:

- Listen to yourself,
- Learn from listening, and
- Alter your conversation, if needed.

It shouldn't take you more than a day to discover into what category most of your conversation falls.

When I conduct a Self-Communication Audit, I put my words in one of two columns:

Uplifting, Supportive, Positive	Destructive, Unkind, Negative

Years ago, during a difficult time, I was surprised when I first did this audit. After only one day of the audit, I found that more than half my conversations were in the negative column. I never realized I made so many unproductive comments. I gossiped, and I often complained, as I played the "why me?" card.

I even noticed that people reciprocated with similar negative remarks in a similar negative tone, supporting mine. If I complained, people listened and then they began to complain, too. I had started a chain reaction of unproductive conversation. I was horrified!

I also noticed what happened to *my* internal energy when I was negative and unkind. My negative remarks may have hurt or bothered others and affected their energy levels, but what my negativity did to me was literally palpable. My energy level plummeted and left me depleted and yearning for some kind of pick-me-up. It became twice as difficult to generate positive thoughts or conversations once I let negativity loose. That's when I made a commitment to change my conversation, for good.

When I realized that being negative submerged and overwhelmed the best I had to offer, I worked daily to minimize gossiping, backbiting, criticizing, and whining. I have no regrets; I'm really glad I made an effort to change this kind of pollution. As I continue to be vigilant about my conversation, I have made a commitment to myself that my new direction in life would help humankind and the world by offering a positive uplifting voice every chance I got. Being positive has become a terrific energizer.

Got problems? Even so, they don't have to generate negativity. Problems can be discussed with the intention of determining the next step toward a solution. We don't have to become negative when we discuss problems. If we stick to the facts of the problem rather than engage in its negative emotional aspects, chances are good we will find a way out. Many good managers have told me, "If you find a problem and want to share it, be sure to come prepared with a few potential solutions."

"I haven't been happy for a long time," Leah told me, "because I was surrounded by a lot of unhappy people. For some reason I thought I could help them. But in the end, helping them just seemed to drag me down. I got depressed. I knew I needed to change something. I also knew I was the one to instigate the change—and that the time was now. Happy people attract happiness. Right now, I'm in a good place. I'm focused and centered. I know what I want for my family and in my career. I'm on the right track."

I agree that we alone have to set our direction and make the changes. Now that most of my days are filled with positive, upbeat, lighthearted people, I have no desire to return to "downer" conversations. Creating this new habit has been life changing for me, and I know I'm on the right track because of a compliment someone recently gave me.

"You know, JJ," Nancy said, "you always find the positive in situations and people. Over the years, I cannot recall hearing you gossip about others. I always feel inspired when I leave our conversation and look forward to the time we can meet again."

I smiled, glad I had made the effort to change—and it *was* an effort. As the results became quickly apparent, the effort became easier. Now, when I want to say something awful to or about someone, I remind myself that my intention is to be a positive force for good in the world.

If you are one of those positive, upbeat, life-giving people who doesn't engage in any of the negative behaviors I've mentioned, good for you. Keep on spreading your good energy. We sure need it.

Watch what you say and how you say it. Be diligent. Determine to be a positive force at home and at work.

After you conduct your Self-Communication Audit, think about posting your results. We all need encouragement, so tell us what you discovered and what you plan to do about it. Let us know how you altered your conversation and what results manifested.

You know how we mute the phone when we're taking another call or when we need to speak to another person? Well, maybe it's time to mute the negative so we can carry on a much different conversation for the rest of our lives: a positive one.

Step 6: Mute the negative.

CHAPTER 16:

Getting Unstuck

It's only when we truly know and understand that we have a limited time on earth—and that we have no way of knowing when our time is up—that we will begin to live each day to the fullest, as if it was the only one we had. ~**Elizabeth Kubler-Ross**

How often do you worry about things you can't change? How frequently do you compare yourself to others who, in some cases, you don't even intimately know?

Our society encourages us to watch what other people do, care about whom they date, and what they wear and eat. How often do you rubberneck? The heavy viewership of reality TV is a perfect example of how much society encourages us to watch others. Consciously or not, we then compare ourselves to others, creating fertile ground for envy, jealousy, and pride. It's no surprise that by focusing on the lives of other people (whether they are celebrities, our neighbors, or our co-workers), we take the focus away from what we need to do to in our own lives. Rather than centering attention on making our own lives fuller and happier, it's easier to sit and watch others. Is it any wonder that we then feel less energetic toward our own, sometimes messy but glorious, lives?

The Working Woman's GPS:
When the Plan to Have It All Has Led You Astray

Go to Inventory D—Dreams & Desires. Pick one thing that gives you energy. Then, pick one television show you always watch or one chore you always do. Instead of watching that show every week or doing that chore (which will always be there), engage one of your dreams instead.

Have you always wanted to join a book club, take a yoga class, study film culture, learn to make pots, begin your CPA, read a certain novel?

Pick a dream or desire and go for it. It isn't that relaxing by watching television is bad; it's that the hardest choices are often between the good and the better. You may be too busy every night and you need to relax one evening. But it's also true that fulfilling one small part of a dream or desire will boost your spirits and your energy even more as you gain skills to make the leap to a more purpose-filled life. What energizes us is a clear indication of purpose.

Habits are hard to break; they are comfortable and manageable, and they often keep us from making choices we know are overdue, whether in a job, a marriage, or a friendship. We stick with what we know and let our fears keep us from risking what it might take to live an inspired life. We become so averse to change, that instead of soaring to the next level, we plod along well beyond the time the job, the marriage, or the friendship has stopped generating positive energy.

How many of your daily feelings around your commitments are marked with a minus (-)? We usually know inside ourselves that we have to change something; we just don't always *want* to know it.

There were many times in my career when I knew it was time to move on, but I was comfortable. There were, after all, things about the job I liked, roles that enabled me to have time for other commitments. But it was time to move on.

When we delay making the change, weeks become years, and we can't get that time back.

Cathy told me how her focus changed. "I never thought when I was fifty, that I would be running my own businesses and be an entrepreneur," she said. "I always thought I would be a global merger acquisitions lawyer and be doing deals until I died. I was a deal lawyer inside and out."

But Cathy knew that she wanted something that matched her values and so she broke out of her comfort zone and risked a new beginning. Staying in a profession that doesn't make you happy will eventually, as Cathy said, make you "terribly, terribly unhappy."

I agree with Cathy. Staying when it's time to go doesn't settle well with our soul, and then, each day, we lose more and more feeling and energy.

"Losing energy and joy," Cathy said, "translates through to your kids. And if they don't *see* passion, they don't live passionately."

Living a passionate life, which comes from focus and meaningful choices, is what it's all about.

Step 7: Stretch beyond your comfort zone.

CHAPTER 17:

Quiet the Inner Critic

Always be a first-rate version of yourself, instead of a second-rate version of somebody else. ~**Judy Garland**

Along with our habit of being inordinately absorbed in other people's lives, we also have a tendency to judge others.

We've all made choices that have resulted in additional responsibilities, and we often don't realize how and where a specific combination of choices might land us. It's pretty true, though, that the choices we've made, perfect or imperfect, have brought us to where we are today. So, there's no reason to judge the choices of others; it is not a great use of our time and energy. Any single choice—to marry or not, to have children or not, to stay home with our children or go to work—is rarely a THIS or THAT decision.

I know working women who long to be home with their children, and I know stay-at-home moms who long to be in the work world. We make choices for reasons that make sense at the time. Why allow society, through television and magazine articles, force us into a conversation about which decisions are right or wrong. Is this helping? Is it advancing anyone? Such programs and articles leave many women uncomfortable and aggravated.

The Working Woman's GPS:
When the Plan to Have It All Has Led You Astray

"Give each other freedom to choose what's best for each of us and let's not compare our lives to what is happening to others," Leslie said. "It can be debilitating. You can see someone who is a natural mother and appreciate that and then see someone who is struggling so much with that same role. I'd really like people to be their own role model and not compare themselves to others. It hurts you and hurts other women. It's not the best and highest purpose for you when you compare yourself to society's expectations."

I've wondered why women choose to participate in "us" versus "them" programs and to respond to such articles. My position is that we need to avoid conversations, programs, and magazines that encourage us to judge others. Each of us has her own perspective and, as we've learned, our perspectives are likely to evolve over the years and so do our choices. Something we never thought we'd do when we were young, we find ourselves doing—and often for a good reason. Trial and error are important life lessons.

"When I was younger and even in high school," Kimberly said, "I would think, maybe I would work even if I did not have to. Then, in college, I considered how nice it would be to be home fulltime in the future [with my children], and I would swing in the other direction. And now that I'm in the working world, I realize that staying home and not working would be an even tougher job for me, personally."

When you find yourself tempted to judge somebody, put the focus back on yourself. Quiet that inner critic and ask the deeper questions:

- Why do I need to judge this person?
- Is there something going on in my life that makes me uncomfortable with this person's choice? Is it something I'm not willing to admit or look at?
- What do we have in common that I haven't recognized?

Unlike our sisters in many parts of the world, we have freedom and many more choices.

Just as Leslie said when she talked to me about her dreams and desires (Chapter 9, Inventory D), we all would benefit by making a commitment to becoming a pioneer in our own life.

By turning our attention to our own lives, ignoring the well-worn rut of focusing on others (reality television, movie star worship, etc.), and refusing to judge, we help stop the negative parade that never goes anywhere.

Let's create our own structures, agendas, and goals as Leslie suggests. Let's become comfortable with our own choices, build our own roads, fill our own buckets, move in new directions if needed, and walk our own paths. Let's live our own lives, without judging ourselves or others. Let's put all we are out there. Let's become pioneers.

Step 8: Refuse to judge.

CHAPTER 18

Before You Say Yes

We are the hero of our own story.
~Mary McCarthy

A bit more about choices but from a different perspective: Even if you haven't accepted my belief that everything that happens is useful and brings us to a place of readiness, it is now time to get poised to accelerate to the next level of your journey.

Sometimes the only choice we have is the attitude we bring to events, relationships, and situations. Let's look at how we handle the choices we do have.

Can you say NO?

Eckhart Tolle is one of my favorite authors. In *The Power of NOW*[13], Tolle writes that there is only ever Now. The past only happened in the Now, and the future--which hasn't happened yet--will only happen in the Now of the present moment. There is only, *ever*, *NOW*, this present moment. Every day we are faced with multiple opportunities to choose. Each of us has twenty-four hours in the Now of each day. How will we spend that time?

---

13   See footnote 6

The Working Woman's GPS:
When the Plan to Have It All Has Led You Astray

I once had a manager who provided a unique lesson on time. Once he finished a meeting or conversation, he would make observations and ask questions, such as: "That is thirty minutes of time that we will never get back. Do you think that was a good use of our time? Should we have spent more or less time on those topics?"

His questions always struck me, and they still resonate with me when I enter someone's office or walk into a meeting. On what do we choose to spend our time? [Time] is clearly one of our most precious and critical assets.

The present moment and the issue of balance belong together. It's not realistic to suggest that we can always achieve balance, yet many women I've interviewed hold it up as a goal they long to accomplish. Some of us may be on an everlasting search to find it.

Leslie suggested we need to find creative ways to stay balanced, to do the things that most energize us, and to reach out to others in need. Sarah M. confessed that she struggles with putting so much time into work—whether by doing the work or worrying about the work—that she frequently feels out of balance.

One way to help us stay balanced is to treat the present moment as our biggest asset. Determine how you will spend the present moment and with whom. Give yourself permission to say "no" when others request your time, especially if you realize it is not an effective and energizing use of your time. Think back to the many lessons in Chapter 14.

Women are notorious for saying *yes* quickly, easily, and often from the heart. Saying *no* even to good causes and initiatives feels selfish, but it isn't. *No* is an important word to have ready. I have met many wonderful women who gave of themselves to others in more ways than they had time to give. These additional demands, although noble, depleted their energy, compromised their best and most genuine self, affected their work and family life, and threw their lives out of balance.

If you are regularly asked to devote your time and energy toward a worthy project or initiative, those requests are not coincidental. We're asked because people know we can get things done. It's an honor to be asked, but we cannot let that ego thrill prevent us from pausing and asking ourselves these kinds of questions: Is this the right thing at the right time for me? If I accept, will I be doing it for the right reasons?

I used to become so excited when asked to lead or participate in a project or charity event; I was thrilled to be asked, and I always said *yes*. I found myself working well into the night trying to meet all expectations. Everyone in my life suffered when I didn't—or couldn't—say a gracious, "No, but thank you for asking me."

Stay present to the now, ask yourself relevant questions *before* you say *yes* to something that might throw you off balance. As we learn to better discern what is ours to do, and what is *not* ours to do, we will better discern our destination.

If you can't say *no* or find a way to decline a request, you will continue to over-commit, thus draining your energy. There are so many good projects and so much that needs to be done; yet helping every cause that needs our help and every person who asks are not necessarily part of our life script. Such decisions require periods of silence and reflection. Otherwise, we do the same-old-same-old: *"Sure!"*, we say. Then we feel depleted. Thus do you—do we all—prevent time from being wisely aligned with our assets.

Society's Plan of keeping inordinately busy doesn't leave a lot of room for saying *no.* But as Dr. Phil likes to ask, "How's that working for you?"

Not very well, most of us will admit.

I've found that I am more successful if I concentrate on a few (usually no more than three) projects at a time. These projects can be a mix of professional, personal, and community initiatives that include my children or family, local and global initiatives around women, and emerging technologies. I'm learning to use my time wisely and to choose projects carefully. One of my overall goals is to motivate and elevate women, so I often say *yes* to these kinds of projects—the ones that are aligned with my assets (Inventory B). If I were less selective, less able to say *no,* if I took on other initiatives, I would deprive myself of the time to do well the projects that most fulfill me.

As S.R. Covey puts it, "The main thing is to keep the main thing the main thing."[14] I actively work to follow that advice. Decide what your "main thing" is, and stick to it.

Before you say *yes,* take time to think deeply about these questions:

---

14   *S. R.Covey, A. Roger Merrill and Rebecca R. Merrill, First Things First. (London: Simon & Schuster, UK Ltd. 1994.)*

- Do I understand how much work is ahead of me and clearly understand what is expected of me?
- Can I list the expectations?
- What other commitments could interfere?
- Is this project in line with my bold goals?
- If I took it on, would it be for the right reasons?
- Would the timing be right?
- What does taking on this project mean to my everyday life? How will it impact my other responsibilities and commitments?
- Who else needs to be involved?
- What would success look like?
- What will suffer if I accept this task?
- Am I the best person for this task?
- Do I need more information before I start?

A more comprehensive list of questions can be found on my blog by searching "Before You Say Yes."

At first I found it difficult to say *no,* but when I started assessing each task against the questions above, I found a sense of personal reward and satisfaction for taking on only those tasks that were in line with my overall goals. And *that* was essential to my overall happiness and success.

Step 9: Use "No".

CHAPTER 19:

The Flow Within

There is only one journey: Going inside yourself.
~**Rainer Maria Rilke**

I've been referring to energy and energy sources throughout this book. Now, it is time to describe what I'm referring to as it relates to many women's journeys.

I recognize energy as particles that flow through my body and ultimately through my life. Energy is noticeable. You can create energy by yourself, get energy from others, take energy away, and give energy back. Life is all about exchanging energy.

Make time for this: Sit in a place that is quiet, peaceful, and relaxing. (You may have to wait until everyone is in bed.) Sit with your feet together touching the floor, your back straight, your head high, and fingertips together in your lap. Essentially, you are making a circle with your body and no one point is alone; you have connected all the limbs.

Now breathe gently and purposefully. Allow your mind to be still—just for two or three minutes. Instead of thinking, focus on your breath, your inhalation and exhalation. After two or three minutes, when you've finished, you can think all you want.

Do this exercise at least once a day for two or three minutes at a time. I think you will begin to sense and to feel the energy flowing inside you. Notice the energy, acknowledge it, and breathe. You are taking these few minutes for *you.*

The goal of this simple exercise is to relate to your breath and the energy inside you. Don't worry if you feel nothing and you get nothing out of the exercise. Try again. If you do it regularly—just two or three minutes at a time and every day—you will soon feel more of a connection to yourself, others, and the Universe.

This exercise also gives you a chance to just *be* for a few minutes, to be *in* your physical body. We aren't often mentally, emotionally, and physically focused on our bodies. It's easy to lose touch with the gift of our own body and all it allows us to do. Become aware of the energies you are holding and the way you move through your day.

There are several books, CDs, and other materials on the practice of meditation that can be very helpful. I have found that meditation has helped me improve my connection to myself and to the Universe as a whole. I am still practicing and learning, but I credit meditation with helping me respect myself and appreciate my body, which makes me feel peaceful and whole.

Leah told me she has found this practice helpful.

"I almost hate to say it again, but, breathe," Leah said. "Breathe, and take a step back. Always do a little something for you."

Step 10: Be still, sit quietly, breathe.

CHAPTER 20

Get Reacquainted

A little of what you fancy does you good.
~Marie Lloyd

Many women tell me that it is impossible for them to get away from their existing demands. I'm amazed at the reasons they give about why they cannot find the time they need to exercise, meet their friends for dinner, or schedule a necessary personal appointment. They have convinced themselves that they are not worthy to spend time alone, that the demands of others are more important. Why do we make life so hard on ourselves?

If you need it, this chapter gives you permission to schedule some time to be with yourself. Put it on your calendar now; start with one hour a week. Putting yourself on your calendar is important and should be considered a must-do every week. I'm reminded about a saying I often hear at motivation forums: Put the Big Rocks in the jar first, and fill in the pebbles and sand around them.

You are a Big Rock.

If you put the pebbles and sand in first, there is no room for the big rocks in the jar. But if you put the big rocks first, there is always room for the pebbles and sand to fill in around the big rocks. So prioritizing your commitments is critical, which means you must treat yourself as a Big Rock.

Understanding that you are a Big Rock and treating yourself as one are independent actions. Commit to yourself and make time for yourself. Then execute!

The time you spend with yourself can be as inexpensive or expensive as you wish. Dentist and doctor appointments don't count for Big-Rock time with yourself. This time needs to be enjoyable and when you finish you should feel positive and re-energized.

If you don't start now, when *will* you start to make yourself a priority? If you spend some time reconnecting with yourself, others around you will benefit, too. I know, there are a million reasons why you can't, but do it anyway. You need time for yourself and you will return more connected and effective. The other pebble and sand commitments will go better if you take care of the big rocks, including yourself, first.

In *Never Eat Alone: And Other Secrets to Success, One Relationship at a Time*[15], Keith Ferrazzi and Tahl Raz recommend eating with others. I often use meals to meet with people who help advance my work, my network, or to catch up with loved ones. However, I find it a real gift when, a few times a month, I can eat alone. I really cherish that time. I began eating alone years ago when I was a road warrior. At first it felt odd to eat alone; I began eating in the bar area and eventually promoted myself into the din-

---

15   *Keith Ferrazzi with Tahl Raz, 2005. Never Eat Alone And Other Secrets To Success One Relationship At a Time. A Currency Book published by Doubleday.*

ing room. Now, when I see people I know, they often look at me as if they feel sorry for me, eating alone. Sometimes, they ask me to join them. I kindly decline their offer, and silently say to myself, *I honor myself with some delicious food and time to be with myself, to reflect.*

To my meals alone, I may bring a list of questions I want to think about or a book I want to read. Sometimes, I just look around and let my mind wander. When I finish, I'm as proud as a peacock because I have honored myself by making time for me.

Our culture has conditioned us to believe that we always have to be with someone, that being alone is to be avoided at all costs. I have found just the opposite to be true. Being alone for some time each week, without any particular demands, is empowering; it creates positive energy in me that I can then share with others.

Leah noted the same thing during her interview. "As women, we always feel that it's selfish to think about ourselves. Do I sneak in for a haircut before they close or do I help put the kids to bed? We have to choose. And we always feel we have to make the right choice, or at least I do. A lot of time what we'd choose comes last, or not at all."

Spending time with your *self* is necessary if you want to connect with your highest energy, which will open doors you never knew existed. Believe me, connecting with your *self* will yield surprising results.

"Inevitably," I said to Gillian, "if you're happy with yourself, the world works a lot better, don't you think?"

Gillian's response was immediate and intuitive: "When you're portraying and exuding positive energy in this world," she said, "you are going to get positive things back."

The Working Woman's GPS:
When the Plan to Have It All Has Led You Astray

If treating yourself to dinner alone is too big a step, then go alone on a visit to a park, garden, art gallery, or museum. Take a walk through a new neighborhood where you are unlikely to get stopped by people you know. Stroll around the mall with the intention to purchase nothing. Rather, listen to the bustle of others' lives and reflect on your own. Look around you; notice what's there. Smile at people. You will find yourself grateful for making it a priority to get reacquainted with your *self.*

When you spend time reacquainting yourself with who you are, you are giving your mind and body a needed break from the influx of people, energies, and situations around you. By physically moving out of a situation that can drain you, you allow the space to separate and get to know and renew yourself. Eventually, as you continue to nourish and honor yourself in these ways, you will become more aware of your inner energy. One day soon, you will be able to sit with your feet touching, head high, and fingertips together, feeling your own energy anywhere, anytime, even in a restaurant; it is your signal of life.

Step 11: Be your own date.

CHAPTER 21:

Preparing to Leap

*How wonderful it is that nobody need wait a single
moment before starting to improve the world.*
~Anne Frank

Are You Investing Time?

Investment time is different. It is not an hour-long date
with yourself, but a few minutes you can grab now and
again to renew and invest in yourself. What do you choose
to do when you find yourself with fifteen minutes alone?
When you have time to spare, how do you spend it? Do
you call a friend, read a book, take a walk, play with the
dog? What activity do you love to do when you can escape
the ever-present "to-do" list, even for a short time?

My mother loves to read books or play memory games
on the computer in the winter and be in her garden in
the summer. These activities calm her mind and renew
her energy. A friend of mine loves to follow fashion and
talk about her last night out and who wore what. Another
friend of mine likes to throw on her running shoes and
enjoy the outdoors. What do you like to do for self-invest-
ment? Experiment and find out which activities create the
greatest amount of self-harmony, calm, and renewed en-

ergy for you. I believe that as we age, we tend to gravitate toward activities that create serenity, allowing us to rest our thoughts and mind.

I asked Shelley, "When you're not working and you're not with your family, how do you spend your time? What do you do for yourself that has nothing to do with being an employee, life partner, daughter and mom?"

Shelley thought a moment. "There's not very much of that time. It's usually in tiny moments. It's not big but tiny moments where it's just me. I usually just sit and reflect."

Go back to Inventory D–Dreams & Desires and find out what dream you might be able to grab a few recess minutes to begin. List five dreams you might begin if you had fifteen, twenty, thirty minutes. Pick the dream that most excites you, that creates the most energy in you. When you have a few minutes, begin it.

For Christy, "It's about learning to capture calmness and a sense of happiness."

You might want to paint the living room: In fifteen minutes you can open the can of paint, spread a drop cloth, and paint a couple of swaths. Maybe one of your desires is to run in the next local race, so you can jog-even in place—for fifteen minutes. You might want to submit an original recipe, short story, essay, or poem to a magazine. In fifteen minutes you can begin the process, print the submission, or look up the address of the magazine. You can lift some hand weights if you want to improve your strength and tone your arms. String those beads, cut that piece of glass, plant one shrub or flower, or sprinkle some seeds on the soil. This exercise is not about tasks, but about dreams.

We usually put our dreams on the back burner, hoping that someday we will suddenly have time for them. I know I do. But if we use those few moments each day to make small investment steps toward a desire, we are more likely to make it a reality while generating some energy. It's one of life's paradoxes: Spending time creating an abundance of positive energy in yourself (instead of focusing solely on the "to-do" list) will likely make you buzz with energy, and we all love to be around people who create and live an inspired life. So when those moments come along, grab them.

Step 12: Invest in yourself.

Ready to Leap?

In this section, you've made small adjustments, some of which you may already have under way. Efforts to incorporate these adjustments into your daily and weekly activities will surely generate additional positive energy. They will strengthen your courage and determination, which are necessary if you want to revise the Plan and advance your journey. Let's review these steps:

1. Cherish your perfect and imperfect self.
2. Start the day by revving your energy.
3. Become contagious—smile.
4. Focus on the positive.
5. Appreciate life's teaching moments.
6. Mute the negative.
7. Stretch beyond your comfort zone.
8. Refuse to judge.
9. Use "No".

10. Be still, sit quietly, breathe.
11. Be your own date.
12. Invest in yourself.

The intention is to provide tools, tactics, and actions that will create positive energy as you go through your daily activities and commitments.

I have used all of these ideas to fuel my own life. These steps have created an abundance of positive energy in and around me, allowing me to use my assets and talents to create my own journey and to manifest a life of inspiration.

It's now definitely time to leap. In the next section, you will revise society's Plan and further develop a Plan of your own choosing that will likely accelerate your journey to include your Goals that are filled with a sense of Purpose and Self.

PART IV:
REFOCUS, RECALCULATE, ACCELERATE

CHAPTER 22:

Assemble a Team

Nobody can go back and start a new beginning,
but anyone can start today and make a new ending.
~Maria Robinson

I hope, by now, you agree that there is a bigger Plan for each of us than the Plan society has told us is the perfect Plan to have it All. The good news is that society's Plan may have accidentally inspired us to desire more, to yearn for an inspired life, and to create a Plan that is more aligned with our best self and what we have to offer.

I believe there *is* a Plan for each of us. I believe that *each of us* must create our own Plan; we must draw our own road map.

Now that you've practiced making small adjustments on a daily basis, you've likely created more positive energy, which will help you shift into a higher gear. Now, it's time to pull out your list of People & Energy from Inventory A. From the list you made, identify the people who can best assist you in developing a new direction toward your own Plan. Get ready to accelerate your journey.

When I reached this point in my journey, I found myself energized, but something was still holding me back from accelerating. I realized that I could not continue to interact in the same way with the same people. I knew intuitively that I needed a group of people who could help guide me safely through the curves in the road ahead, around the detours, and to my destination.

As you reflect on the people you've listed in Inventory A, you may choose to invite only a few people from your list who will help you create a revised Plan. Select people who you feel will best help you ignite your energy and put YOU into a higher gear as you re-route and recalculate your journey.

Use your inventories to make a list of possible candidates for your team. If someone on your list didn't score a plus (+) in all the categories of the inventory (Inventory A), continue to love them and be a friend, but please don't put them on your team, at least for now.

Minimizing the time you engage with the people with a minus (–) sign after their names—for now—will give you some time to connect with other people who might bring more positive energy and guidance to your team. This is an important recommendation because often we hold on to relationships long after the positive impact has ended. Give yourself permission to let these people go so you can open this space for people who have the ability to offer you more positive influence and guidance.

I call the people I assembled my "board of directors." Some call this group an "inner circle," "a trusted network," or "my team of advisors." The name is not as important as their function: a handful of people within your inner circle upon whom you call for advice and guidance.

Assemble a Team

By establishing a good team—my board of directors—I get great input and feedback. My board brings me ideas I need and guidance I value. They pump me up when I'm down and celebrate with me when I succeed.

According to Wikipedia,[16] "a board of directors is a body of elected or appointed members who jointly oversee the activities of a company or organization. The body sometimes has a different name, such as board of trustees, board of governors, board of managers, or executive board. It is often simply referred to as 'the board.'

"A board's activities are determined by the powers, duties, and responsibilities delegated to it or conferred on it by an authority outside itself." *That authority is YOU.* "These matters are typically detailed in the organization's bylaws, which also commonly specify the number of members on the board, how they are to be chosen, and when they are to meet."

Seem silly? After all, a board of directors is geared to a company, not to an individual, right?

I'm asking you to think about *yourself* as a company. Just as boards usually guide a company on the verge of making a big decision, so will the team you assemble guide you. A board also acts as another level of accountability, meaning they will help keep you on track to reach your goals.

Perhaps you're aware that you already have an informal or "default" board of directors, whether or not you call them that. They are the people you call upon when you need to discuss something urgent or especially exciting,

---

16   http://en.wikipedia.org/wiki/Board_of_Directors

when you feel really good or really bad about something. For obstacles with a spouse or partner, you may go to one or two friends; concerns with your children, you may go to an aunt or to a sister; decisions at work, you might gravitate to an entirely different group of people. Whoever they are, your "default" board listens to you, gives advice, tells you what they think you should—or should not—do, suggests ways to handle challenging situations, advises you on career moves, financial matters, fashion decisions,, and other sundry decisions. Your default board could be family members, in-laws, boss, co-workers, friends, spiritual director, minister, or therapist. They are the people around you who have the most to say about your activities, duties, and responsibilities. Most of them should show up on Inventory A.

It's important to know who is on your "default" board so you can create and establish a team with great impact. How did each member of your default board score on Inventory A? If they got all plus (+) signs, it's pretty certain they will stay on your formal board.

The Plan for your life can be as big or small as you want to make it; each choice will be critical. A board or team helps with your GPS; they send out traffic alerts and pull out a compass when needed. They notify you about what the weather will be, where to avoid congested areas, and what highways are congested or under construction. A board provides route suggestions. A team like this is invaluable.

Don't be surprised if some people think it's odd that you want to establish a formal board of directors. Sometimes they won't understand. That's why it's important to discuss your goals and ideas with people you're considering for the board. Share what you are trying to do and your reasons why. Give them the opportunity to decide if they want to help you. Don't waste a seat on someone who, for any number of reasons, is either not interested or doesn't seem to take you and the idea of a board seriously.

Some of my board members have been in my life since my early childhood. Other people I've met along the way have brought positive energy, great advice, and synergy into my life. My board members are tremendously valuable in multiple ways: they help me discern what I need to do now to accomplish my goals and help me choose what can be tabled until later. They're always there to lend an ear and provide great perspective about the topic at hand. Some of them send articles, ideas, and job opportunities to me; they are very proactive on my behalf. Others are reactive; they are always available to respond when I need to confirm my direction.

Selecting a team or board may seem odd, but I offer a few suggestions about choosing board members best suited to guide you as you accelerate.

First, set a bold goal to hand-pick the highest quality people. Don't let guidance for such an important step fall to a default board of people who happen to be in your life due to marriage, family of origin, where you attend church, or where you work. Make sure that every single person belongs on your team.

Start by thinking of some scenarios: If you had great news to share or a problem to solve, whom would you call?

Are these the same people you would call to discuss a work issue, a community issue, or a hurdle with your children?

Second, ideally, your board should have people from different areas and with various viewpoints; don't get caught up with titles. Your mother-in-law may be a better choice than your sister. Your minister may be perfect—or not—for your board. It's up to you. Take time to look at your list from Inventory A and place it alongside your default board. Sit with it. Breathe. Ask yourself these questions as you reflect on who you will assemble for your team:

- Who are my champions?
- Who will best guide me?
- Who will support me as I blossom, as I evolve?
- Who will feel uncomfortable about my plan or possibly sabotage it?
- What gaps do I have on my team?
- Who can I assist on her/his journey?

Board members should not only be supportive and encouraging—ideally they will have your best interests at heart and will ask you effective questions.

Many times, my board has actively stepped in to guide me to a decision without making it for me. At times, they've encouraged me to re-think a decision or choice. Sometimes, they've steered me back on track when I was about to run off course.

Third, don't limit yourself to assembling just one board. For example, I have three boards: A Family Board for my roles as mother, wife, sister, daughter, godmother, and related roles; a Career Board for everything that has to do with my career; and a Motivational Board related to my passion for motivating and inspiring women.

My husband, my mother, and my two best friends sit on each of my three boards; they are the most important, influential, and highly energetic, good people in my life.

If I have issues I need to address about my family, I add my sisters-in-law and my neighbors to the board; together my board members' voices of reason, skill, and compassion really help guide me when obstacles appear or I need advice.

If I want to talk about my career in technology, then to those top four people I add a former boss, a few co-workers, a past business partner, a past co-worker, and a serial entrepreneur.

Finally, boards should be customized and effective. If you discover you have a knowledge gap on your board, you need to fill it. For example, for my career board, I was lacking a senior technology executive who had years beyond me in experience, perspective, and knowledge. I needed some senior mentoring and career planning advice and guidance.

I had to make a conscious effort to find people with these credentials and then find a way to get to know them so I could determine if there was synergy and mutual respect between us. Through my network, I identified two gentlemen who both had what I needed to fill this board position. I created opportunities to meet each of them; after one year, it was obvious to me which one would make an excellent addition to my board. At that point, I formally asked him to be on my board of directors. He smiled, said he had heard of mentors but not a board of directors for individuals. I told him that his role would be similar to that of a mentor; I explained that six people from various backgrounds make up my board. I've met many of them throughout my career. I emphasized that these people were and are of great benefit to me, and often, I to them.

He then happily agreed to be on my board. He even praised me for formalizing the process and outlining my goals so he could effectively participate in my journey.

Through this process, I learned that what is monitored and measured gets improved and what is celebrated and rewarded gets done. By sharing my goals with people I admire and respect, I created a formal monitoring system. My reward is that I get to share my accomplishments with the very people who helped guide me.

Watch for the people you need by being aware of your daily interactions. Ask the Universe to send you the person you need. Be watchful; he or she is soon likely to appear.

Be proactive in selecting your board. The more active you are in selecting and inviting people, the more effective you, and they, will be. They will take the role of assisting you in this life more seriously, and so will you. You choose how many boards you need and how many people you will invite to sit on each board. Sometimes, the same people will sit on more than one board, but not always. You decide. You also decide what you want each board to do for you.

As my journey from society's Plan to a handmade Plan has evolved, I've experienced numerous rest stops, wrong turns, and joy rides along the way. As I learn to live more and more in the present moment and become more aware of my energies, thoughts, and feelings, I've begun to trust myself more.

I've come to appreciate that life's journeys are not always easy, and change can be unexpected and often difficult. We get stuck along the way; we slip into a rut or a ditch; our energy goes flat. Even heading smoothly in a new direction, I've experienced disappointment and discouragement. But journeys don't end; they just keep on changing. Change is the one sure thing.

As I have evolved, so have my boards. I'm delighted to find myself participating more often on other people's boards as they readjust their journeys. I am delighted and energized by this reciprocity.

Cathy, the global acquisitions lawyer who is now an Episcopal priest and entrepreneur, commented on how she wished she had had a board of directors or a mentor to coach her when she was a young lawyer. "Here I am nearly fifty, and there weren't any women to watch and learn from as I was moving through my career. I was it. I was the only woman sitting at the table negotiating deals in London. There might have been forty people working on deals, and I was the only woman. And so there weren't women I could watch. I think it's important for young women and professionals to find someone who is working or has worked extremely well in their own profession or business and just role model. That's how men have done it for years. They go to the bar, they go to the country club, they go on the golf course, and you can see the young guys' role modeling on the older guys; they're teaching them how to relate."

I asked Paulette what she would look for in a mentor to participate as a member of her board.

"Sincerity, track record, truth, somebody who believes in truth versus harmony. My mentors reinforced the truth even if it wasn't something I wanted to hear. I remember one mentor—he was a terrific mentor—but he was very, very demanding. He knew what I needed to do and he didn't care if I liked him or not. He'd share what I needed to do, and I'd take his advice because he had a track record.... . Honestly, if mentors don't have a track record themselves, you don't know if you can rely upon their advice."

Today, following retirement, Paulette is an entrepreneur and a mentor with the Girl Scouts of America, working with young girls, helping foster future leaders.

If you have people in your life who have been good role models or mentors, tell them so. Tell them how glad you are that they have been there for you. Invite them to be on your board to help you revise the Plan as you evolve your life journey. Tell them the Plan may include a scary but energizing initiative, turning a beloved hobby into a new career, or any number of other ideas dear to your heart.

Remember, most people like to help. Don't make the mistake I initially made: I didn't ask for help because I didn't want to burden anyone; I assumed everyone was overcommitted.

Most people will tell you whether they have the time and interest to join your team. Also, assume that when you ask people to help you that they or someone else will ask for your help. It is a reciprocal world. Be prepared and ready to help others evolve, too.

By nature, journeys undergo continuing refinement. You will always need people to turn to, because journeys have hills and valleys, sharp curves in the road, potholes, and obstacles. You may need to reconstruct your board several times.

Assemble a Team

The good news is that remarkable people will come and go in your life for different reasons and at different times. If you feel fortunate when they are in your life and you work to build bonds that create mutual energy, you will be sure to focus on the opportunity and not the loss when they have to move on. Like you, they too may have big dreams and desires. Wish them well. Encourage them to enjoy the ride.

CHAPTER 23:

Contribute Beyond Your Sphere

I have found that among its other benefits,
giving liberates the soul of the giver.
~**Maya Angelou**

As we claim our path, the next action that can catapult us in a more fulfilling direction is to consider how and in what ways we can give of ourselves beyond our customary sphere of interactions. I'm suggesting that we create opportunities to reach out to the broader world, to make a difference in at least one life outside of our regular circle. I have learned that when we give, we also receive.

The best way to give is when we are in harmony with ourselves, when we can stand in our own truth and share our passion, because then others are often attracted to these engaging energies. Don't we all know when someone has created a life of inspiration? Can't we feel it? Aren't we often attracted to those people and the energies they share with others?

As passionate, harmonious women, we can become a launching pad for others. We can share our time, money, assets, skills, and talents. When we contribute our assets to and for others, they often thrive—and so do we—in unexpected ways. Acts of giving manifest positive energy within us and others, and that energy extends into the world around us—the ripple effect.

My husband, who is truly one in a million for many reasons, is a pro when it comes to doing for others. He has been my inspiration in this area since we met.

"We hit the jackpot in this life, JJ," he constantly reminds me. "So let's focus on sharing with those who didn't get as many advantageous opportunities."

He prides himself on giving of his time and money to help people in need year-round. He enjoys sharing life's gifts with others to help them in their own journeys.

I'm continuing to evolve and truly savor the energy I receive from these moments. We contribute financially to good causes and to foundations that support worthwhile projects. I've found that sharing from my heart and by giving of my energy, time, and knowledge has been more transformative for me than giving money.

I've come to understand a peculiar truth: What we do to ourselves we do to others, and what we do to others we do to ourselves. Writing a check is a wonderful offering, but giving from within is even more demanding and ultimately more rewarding. To my way of thinking, sharing what we have with others is a critical step in reaching a satisfying destination of fulfillment.

I love what Deepak Chopra, M.D., writes in *The Law of Dharma:*[17] "There is something that you can do bet-

---

17   *Deepak Chopra, 1994. The Seven Spiritual Laws of Success: A Practical Guide to the Fulfillment of Your Dreams. San Rafael, CA: Amber-Allen Publishing, New World Library. 60. Online at Share Guide: The Holistic Health Magazine and Resource Directory. "Fulfilling Your Dreams through the Seven Spiritual Laws of Success." Law Seven: The Law of "Dharma" or Purpose in Life. http://www.shareguide.com/Chopra.html*

ter than anyone else in the whole world—and for every unique talent and unique expression of that talent, there are also unique needs. When these needs are matched with the creative expression of your talent, that is the spark that creates affluence. Expressing your talents to fulfill needs creates unlimited wealth and abundance."

Think about your assets, skills, and talents: what can you offer? Figure out some small way you can share yourself so that others might benefit, even if it is only one other person. Can you lend a hand, an ear, a skill, some time, or some funds to advance another's goals or to meet another's need?

Begin with things you can do every day: a smile, a purposeful conversation in which your voice, tone, and focus are on others. If you are currently crunched for time, writing a check does help many charities accomplish amazing results. If you can't offer a donation, think of ways to extend your assets (Inventory B) to others. Are you a good organizer? Are you great at brainstorming ideas or solving problems? Do you like to design a room, a flower arrangement, or a financial plan? You may be the person who has the patience to work with small children or the compassion to work with the sick and dying. Can you raise money with your outgoing personality or your grant writing skills? Is there a school in your neighborhood that needs a tutor for a child? Can you volunteer to help cook or serve a meal to the homeless of your community once a month? Once a year?

One of the best parts of extending ourselves is noticing *how* we do it. *How* will you share? *How* will you feel about spending your time, your assets, talents, and money? Will your heart be in it? Will you look forward to the opportunity? Or will you feel like you "should," but you don't really want to?

I didn't believe I had time to reach out to others—until I did. I was surprised to find that helping others decreased my own "monumental" issues and allowed me to emerge into a more fulfilling life.

For example, I often bring in lunch for working sessions. I often add an extra lunch for the secretary or security guard or person who maintains the grounds. When we host seminars, I often provide a few pro-bono tickets to women who are struggling financially and need a little extra help getting to the next level.

We all need help at some point in our lives. Just as other women have been there for me, I work to elevate women I don't know in a variety of ways. As a natural connector of people, I use my skills and assets to help others find jobs, change jobs, begin initiatives, and find funding. I'm proud of the network I've been able to create and maintain because it has helped so many people along their journeys. Looking beyond myself has brought me much joy.

Get creative and merge multiple initiatives into a focus on giving. Here are some ways my husband and I incorporate our commitment to give into our already busy lives:

- We take our young children to a variety of community initiatives, including food drives or fund-raisers, where tiny hands are welcome to aid their effort.

- We buy tables for charities or fund-raising events and invite our friends to join us. Once there, we catch up with friends and they can learn about the cause.
- We host events at our house for good causes and ask friends to bring donations, if they choose.

There are many creative ways to use your time, assets, and money effectively to benefit good causes.

It's important to treat yourself well and at times, focus solely on yourself. But that self-focus can become myopic if you become too busy to share what you have with someone in need. If you find yourself too busy to do *something* for someone else, maybe you're just *too* busy.

Step back and refocus. Create a space in which you *can* give. Choose wisely and be conscious of your other commitments. Remember to establish good boundaries, which are essential if we are not to become overwhelmed. Too many commitments will prevent us from effectively helping anyone.

When you begin to give, you will find that your life evolves in ways you could never imagine. We are all in this together and as we begin to help others, we find our own path gains clarity. Assess what you have to offer. Assess the time you can give. Then look outward and choose a way to share your gifts.

It's a wonderfully satisfying and important part of the journey!

CHAPTER 24

Dig for Your Nuggets

Life shrinks or expands in proportion to one's courage.
~**Anais Nin.**

Let's circle back and go digging for nuggets we have buried because for too long we've had too many items on our to-do lists, too many responsibilities, and too many tangled threads.

We can easily get lost in the daily grind of tasks that we need to complete from sunrise to sunset. I began to realize that I created my to-do list and much of what was on that list was meant for people I dearly loved; it came with the roles I had accepted.

When I ask these next few question, don't "think" about them. Instead say the first thing that comes to mind. Say it out loud. Or grab a pen and write it down. Ready?

- What do you really enjoy doing?
- What work did you always dream you would do once you became an adult? Why?
- What do people most often ask you to do?

Revisit your list of questions on Inventory D. Do they match? Any surprises? Do you see any common themes?

I ask you to revisit these questions quickly because sometimes, when you are least expecting such questions, the answers that arise in your mind are more instinctual, unconscious, and accurate. Nuggets of truth are often buried deep and may need several excavations (reflections and questions) to reveal themselves.

Identify a nugget of truth about your true desires, even if you cannot deal with that nugget right now. At least excavate it. You can always put it on the shelf for awhile. Any nugget you unearth is a signal to guide you. Hold the nugget of truth in your hand or heart or mind: let it become a touchstone for what fuels your life and thrills your soul.

If you prefer not to dig up one nugget of truth about your deepest desires, ask the significant people in your life to tell you what they see as your most natural gift or talent. Better yet, meet individually with your board members or as a group; ask them to identify your natural assets. When they accepted a board position, they essentially signed up for this type of guidance. Be open and document their feedback. Look back to Inventory D and identify any common themes.

If you love to paint but you paint in secret and have never showed your paintings to anyone, no one will bring up that nugget. People can only provide feedback about assets of which they are aware. Only you can dig really deep for those nuggets you've sequestered in an underground cave for years.

When I asked Christy if there was something she always wanted to do, something outside her comfort zone, something that she'd have to get real gutsy to do, she said, "Yes, but it's so deep I don't know what it is, yet. That's what I'm trying to figure out." Christy is digging for nuggets.

Holly has already dug up one of her deep nuggets of truth. "Actually, I'm more into nature and the outdoors," she told me. "Everyday I wonder why I'm in Cleveland and standing behind this stylist's chair. Whether it's creating a new trail in Appalachia or moving to the ocean and taking my morning jog at the beach, that's been on my mind a lot. I wonder why I'm not there and doing the same thing I'm doing here. And what's stopping me."

To identify and name her nuggets of truth, Leah goes with her gut feeling. "At the end of the day, I want to say that I've done something for me. For a good part of my life, I've done things to please other people; their happiness came first. But I found a mentor who offered to coach me. We talked. Well, I talked most of the time and she listened. She could see that I was passionate and driven, but that I lacked real focus. For what I needed, I wasn't in the right job or the right frame of mind. I wasn't using what I have in me. She pushed me to write down specific goals and to be accountable. She forced me into committing to me."

When I began doing this work, I realized that some of the nuggets that excited me most were focused on initiatives to help, guide, educate, or advance people, especially women. My heart would begin to race with excitement whenever I came in contact with such projects.

I joined the National Speakers Association in my early twenties because I was drawn to people who could motivate others. I attended their Atlanta meetings once a month, although I rarely engaged in the conversation because I was nearly twenty years junior to any other attendee. But the association and their goals fascinated me; I loved to watch and learn.

The Working Woman's GPS:
When the Plan to Have It All Has Led You Astray

Excitement is an indicator of a buried nugget. When you feel excitement, notice what's happening. Admit it to yourself. Then dig for it.

"I was meant to help others" Sharon said. "I know it's not me, it's just knowledge I've been given - or whatever it is I've been given. It's a gift. It's not me; it's just coming through me of what I'm supposed to offer. And, when I am able to do that, that's what makes me happy. It isn't about money or a pat on the back. It's all about making a difference in somebody's life and when I see that, when I feel that from other people, I feel complete."

Listen for nuggets of truth about your desires even if you are struggling with finances, cannot find daycare, or don't have support from the people around you. When we dig for our nuggets and pull them forward and hold them, listen to them, amazing things can and do happen.

Cathy, Christy, Crickett, and Paulette dug up a nugget and became successful entrepreneurs.

Do yourself a favor: Dig up a nugget or two. Hold them inside you. Then start to include at least one of them on your to-do list. For a few minutes every day, treat that nugget as a priority. Don't expect perfection from yourself; just engage a nugget for a few minutes a day. Avoid negativity.

If you think you can or you think you cannot, your destiny will unfold as you predict.

CHAPTER 25

How I Maneuvered My Assets

One needs something to believe in, something for which one can have whole-hearted enthusiasm. One needs to feel that one's life has meaning, that one is needed in this world. ~**Hannah Senesh**

Continually, messages are coming to us. We'll notice them if we pay attention and listen. Opportunities will come to use our assets and to engage our desires and dreams if we can be mindfully in the present moment. Being present to each moment is how we recognize the messages. In the past, I may have called these messages "coincidences," but I have found them to be so much more.

To understand these "coincidences" as the messages from the Universe that I've come to believe they are, I had to acknowledge that I had made some choices that led me astray. Almost every choice I made at this point in my life seemed opposite to my intuition, and although I knew I was being led astray, I was not sure how to reverse it.

Shortly after moving to a new town with my new husband and finding myself without a job, I declined a new position that would have had me traveling most of the week. Initially I felt excited because I thought a short break from my road warrior lifestyle would be good for me, giving me time to settle into my new city and participate in local initiatives. Yet after a few weeks, my energy began to plummet; I didn't know what to do or how to stop the energy loss. I hadn't realized that I had so much pride invested in my work and the network of friends I left behind. I loved the bigger city I had come from and I sorely missed the positive energy of my life in Atlanta.

Since I was still operating under society's Plan, marriage was expected. I thought I could easily rebuild my life in my new city. I wasn't aware of how important it would be to quickly replace the energy sources I left behind. So I coasted for a bit, slowly slipping away from the woman I had been. As weeks and months passed, I began to withdraw from social engagements. My husband, who knew that normally I loved meeting new people, suggested that I go see a doctor. As stubborn as I am, I eventually went to the doctor, who diagnosed me as "depressed" and referred me to a specialist.

During my initial visit, I spent the hour talking with him about my life, including its milestones to date, childhood events, and relationships. In a funny way, recalling key milestones and events in my life gave me energy. Yet as fast as I spoke of my past life and felt the brief high, I was just as quickly into my now-familiar angst again. At the end of the session, the specialist wrote me a prescription for depression, blaming my depression on a "woman's hormones." I laugh now because it's such a "catch-all" phrase.

I was unsatisfied with the diagnosis and as yet unaware of the source of my angst. I took the medication for a few weeks, becoming more and more frustrated with myself and the woman I had allowed myself to become. I'm sure my husband wondered where the woman he proposed to had gone. Finally, I reached the point of "enough's enough" with "poor ole me." I yearned to return to the *me* I used to admire, the me who literally jumped out of bed in the morning.

I became more and more convinced that the root of my depression lay not in my hormones but in the situation that had developed based on the choices I had made. Taking a break from the fast-paced work environment initially seemed like a good plan, but the hiatus zapped my energy; I hadn't yet learned about energy sources.

That's when I began to inventory my life. I talked with my friends and family (who were not yet members of my formal board). They gave me excellent feedback; they told me that I was disconnected from life because my primary assets, which were connecting people, beginning projects, and solving problems were no longer part of my daily life. I had released them haphazardly.

I listened to their feedback, made some of the small adjustments I recommended in PART III: Revising the Course, Building Confidence, set some goals, and began striving toward them.

Using my husband's network, I arranged a meeting with a local nonprofit that I discovered from an online posting needed help with their technology projects. I requested a meeting with the manager. She agreed to meet with me for twenty minutes. During that time, we reviewed a few of her more immediate technology concerns, and then she closed the conversation with "I have little budget."

The Working Woman's GPS:
When the Plan to Have It All Has Led You Astray

I quickly responded, "Pay me for ten hours and I'll work another ten hours free." I think she thought I was either crazy or overselling my skills, but she agreed to the offer since she was desperate; admittedly, so was I.

After working with her for a month, she began referring me to people in her network and before I knew it I was overwhelmed with requests. Since I was interested in building my own network of contacts in my new city, I charged a minimal amount, which seemed to be a big hit around town. One thing led to another; by using and leveraging my knowledge and technology skills, there I was: an independent technology consultant.

After only six months of using my husband's network to secure my first technology project, I had my own network of contacts. I admit it was uncomfortable—and not always easy—to force myself to go alone to events where I knew no one. But I did it, and by taking such bold steps, I built my own network.

One day, in between projects, I stopped at the local community college. My passion for next-generation technology work force drove me there because I heard they were looking for instructors. After a few forms and one interview, I began teaching evening classes on databases. I continued my consulting technology work during the day.

Once I got a few evening classes under way, I began to develop a rapport with some of the students. They told me how difficult it was to land internships, which had a direct impact on their chances of being hired for a full-time technology job because most companies require new hires to have at least some related work experience.

As I grew closer to these students, I began to worry about their career paths. During the day, I primarily assisted small businesses, nonprofits, and entrepreneurs with their technology projects, and one day as I was working on a customer's computer network, I began to connect the dots!

I realized with a flash of insight that I could now connect my students to my Rolodex of contacts. One-by-one, I began to connect the students to small businesses that I knew needed help with various technology projects, including web and logo design, desktop upgrades, and wireless network installation, to name a few. I knew from my experience that many entrepreneurs, small businesses, and nonprofits have limited budgets. Often, these businesses could not make the financial commitment to bring a college student into their business for a two-month or longer internship. However, these same businesses have budgets for *specific* projects, which can vary in length from two hours to more than a month.

The idea of connecting tech-savvy college students to small businesses and nonprofits on a part-time basis not only made financial sense, but it also helped these soon-to-be-graduates develop their skills for the work force. Most college students enjoy part-time work while they concentrate on classes. I saw that they could work on a variety of short technology projects while they gained relevant experience and developed references.

Many of the projects were performed remotely, which created new opportunities for both students and businesses. Once I saw the potential, I knew I needed an automated process to connect my students with the right projects. I worked with one of the tech students to create an electronic forum (TechStudents.net) that connected businesses seeking affordable technology resources with skilled technology students eager to gain real-world experience on an hourly basis.

At its height, it represented technology students from more than three hundred thirty-six colleges, universities, and vocational schools nationwide. It was affordable and effective and it created a win-win for students and small businesses.

TechStudents.net was featured in national and regional publications, such as *Entrepreneur Magazine,* and on online media, including Fast Company's Online Weblog, and Ladies Who Launch.

This was a wonderful, surprising experience that rejuvenated me. I was inspired again because I learned to use my assets. I was alive again. It was worth all those uncomfortable weeks and months of angst to finally rediscover my energy sources.

Admittedly, my move from Atlanta was a scary time, at least initially, but I'm still glad I followed my heart and married a great life partner. That choice took me out of my comfort zone and forced me to re-create myself. Through my loss of self, I had to ask myself the tough questions and search for the answers. Painful and difficult as it was at times, I do not regret taking that leap of faith.

In the process, almost as an added bonus, I learned something important about myself: TechStudents.net was a clear indicator of my assets. I was, and continue to be, a good connector, self-starter, and problem-solver. I found ways to leverage my network of resources so that others could benefit. I also learned that small, local solutions can evolve into national solutions with global influence. I did not make this leap alone. I leaned on many people and on my board of directors to help me along the way.

Coming to the point of self-acknowledgment, I understood that I needed to readjust my lens. Now, years after I started TechStudents.net, I'm still asked to participate in national and international meetings on technology, women in technology, "brain drain", and the next-generation technology work force that will make its mark on U.S. competitiveness globally.

TechStudents.net was a launching pad for bigger and more complex projects. Had I not worked through the inventories, made small adjustments, dug for my nuggets, formed a board of directors, and given of my assets freely, I would not have recognized and acted upon the opportunity before me. I shiver to think I might have allowed that critical opportunity to pass untouched.

I've moved on from this endeavor, but I will always cherish it for advancing my journey, for helping me accelerate.

I discovered that when I made bold choices, I appreciated and respected myself more. Bold choices enhanced my marriage and eventually gave me the inner peace to actively embrace motherhood. Eight years later I have two beautiful children whom I cherish; I learn from them every day.

In addition to the life coaching that opened my mind and encouraged me to look at life with a different lens, another motivation for this book occurred as I thought about my daughter. I wanted to put down my thoughts about society's Plan so I could one day share it with her. I wanted to alert her to the potential pitfalls as well as the successes of women who came before her as they maneuvered their assets to create a life of inspiration.

Embrace the journey regardless of the location because we all have times when we are led astray. Accept that you will make ill choices which may redirect you. Stay strong and know that you have the internal strength to change even though you sometimes want to quit on yourself.

You may not be in technology. You may have made different choices and treasure very different assets than mine, but regardless of our differences, I can assure you that there are opportunities everywhere. You, too, have the exact assets and attributes and nuggets of truth needed to make a difference. Now.

> *The purpose of life is to discover your gift; the meaning of life is to give it away.*
> **~Author Unknown**

CHAPTER 26:

It Is Time

*We will discover the nature of our particular genius
when we stop trying to conform to our own or to other
people's models, learn to be ourselves, and allow our
natural channel to open.* ~**Shakti Gawain**

It is your turn to go in your own direction, to define
your own Plan, and to create your own All for this life.
Now that you know where you are starting from, take your
re-discovered nuggets, your improved energy, and the lessons you've learned, and evolve your journey.

It is time to say farewell to the existing route of pre-
scribed behaviors and to accelerate to a destiny that has
been waiting for you all along.

You are the driving force. You will determine how fast
or slow you will move to a redefined destination and how
quickly you will leverage your fresh perspective to create a
new path.

When your journey ends, how will you have impacted
this world? How will this world describe your life in terms
of the

- **G**oals you have achieved that leveraged your assets
  (nuggets)

The Working Woman's GPS:
When the Plan to Have It All Has Led You Astray

- *P*urpose you drove into this world, and
- *S*elf you brought forward that exuded inspiration.

This is your time, your chance, your choice to give a gift to future generations of women (and men) including your daughters, granddaughters, nieces, daughters-in-law and all the women after you: the gift of stepping outside what others expect, beyond what other people think you should do, and follow your deepest wisdom to create a path of your own choosing.

It is Time.

The road to success is not crowded because while most are looking for ways to take, the truly successful people are finding ways to give. With a giving attitude, every situation is an opportunity for success.

~Author Unknown

ADDENDUM A:
THE WOMEN

Inspirations

Women are fascinating. What women have encountered, endured, accomplished, and commemorated is truly remarkable. I have true appreciation and gratitude for all the women who have come before us and have enabled our lives to be filled with freedom, a voice, and respect. Their sacrifices and determination have provided us the ability to choose a life of our making. We owe it to ourselves and the next generation to contribute to this progression.

Every woman in the world could add another level of insight and advice to this piece of work. The stories are transformational.

Thank you to all the women who have made this book possible. Your choices, insight, and perseverance demonstrate that all of us can alter direction, triumph over setbacks, and make bold choices.

There were hours of memorable and insightful material. With so many nuggets of information across so many perspectives, here is another look at the amazing women who contributed to this book. (Alphabetical)

The Working Woman's GPS:
When the Plan to Have It All Has Led You Astray

CATHY
- Forty-nine, two children, single
- Long-time acquisitions lawyer, now Episcopal priest and president of a green technology company

"I am a single, professional woman. I have raised my kids on my own since they were seven and eight. Now they are seventeen years old and about to be sixteen .... So I have done it myself. And I have said 'we are a team,' and I have been very frank with them that, for me to support the things that we believe are important in my family, which is the education of my children, their active participation in competitive sports, things that we believe are really important and we love to do, I have explained to them that I have to work to support us in the way that I do. And we have very open conversations about what they need me at and what they don't, and where they really want me, and where they really don't need me. When they were little and couldn't articulate, I would make the best choices I could that seemed to matter. Now the way I do it so that I don't have guilt, is I have my children involved in the decision making."

CHRISTY
- Thirty-eight, married, three children
- Vice-president, now a Public Relations Consultant

"It's about finding pride in what you do and knowing that's the ultimate important thing in your life...feeling like you get up every day with a purpose that helps you get through the day and that's exactly what you want to do. . . . It's about learning to capture calmness and a sense of happiness, and not have the feeling like it's a step backward. That's where I'm at right now. I left a corporate job and feel I should probably get another corporate job. But for right now, I'm spending time with my family. That's actually a step forward that I need to embrace."

CRICKETT
- Fifty-nine, married, two children
- Held many jobs before becoming an entrepreneur

"I kind of have an unusual journey because I've had a number of careers. I got married when I was twenty-six and I didn't have children for five years because I've traveled all over the world.... And I am a former foster child, so I could have no way envisioned having a child during that period of time. I was pretty certain I wanted to have kids, I just didn't know when."

The Working Woman's GPS:
When the Plan to Have It All Has Led You Astray

GILLIAN

- Twenty-five, single
- Public Relations

"I have a family wedding at the end of May so I'm curious to learn what their reaction will be. I'm wondering if people will be asking me, 'Oh, Gillian, when will you be finding a nice boy and settling down?' Right now I'm thinking I could potentially be letting them down but what I'm learning is that that doesn't really matter. . . . What's helped me is cultivating some really, really close friends. I've networked a group of people here in Chicago that I really enjoy and trust. I've learned to be so strong. I've learned you don't necessarily need all the boxes checked off because life can be great, even if they're not."

HOLLY

- Thirty-eight, married, no children
- Premier Hairstylist

" I'm looking for more spiritual goals–sort of reconnecting with something I lost a long time ago, something that I had when I was younger and left to the wayside. I'm trying to figure that out, a little bit more . . . . That's where I'm at, right now."

KIMBERLY
- Twenty-four, single
- Left Finance/Banking for Medical Equipment Sales

"It is the successes that drive me. Achieving one success motivates me to achieve another one and then another one; I want to do it again and again.. . . . I want to live the legacy my parents have: find a career I'm passionate about; marry a man who challenges me, elevates my thinking, supports me in pursuing my dreams; and then, pass that mentality on to my children. If my parents did it, why can't I achieve it all?"

LEAH
- Thirty-two, married, two children
- Director of Communications

"I want it all. . . . You know, you can have it all. You just may not have it all right now. I put that into perspective and I try to let that lead me, to give me direction in life and give me purpose."

The Working Woman's GPS:
When the Plan to Have It All Has Led You Astray

LESLIE
- Thirty-nine, married, no children
- Entrepreneur

"I definitely felt pressure and I always felt like an oddball for not having kids. I always thought I wasn't going to. I got a lot of family pressure from that. . . . Fortunately, my husband is agreeable. So I don't feel pressure from him. I don't feel pressure really from women or other folks, but I still feel somewhat an oddity. When someone asks if I have kids and I say no, they feel uncomfortable and self-conscious for having asked."

PAULETTE
- Sixty-three, married, two children
- Vice-president, telecommunications industry (retired); Entrepreneur

"One of the things I was able to do was when I was at work, I was at work. I was dedicated to the workplace. Same with being at home–when I was at home, I was focused being at home. Sunday night was always a challenge for me—always—because I had to transition from one spot to the other."

SARAH M.

- Thirty-four, married, two children
- Healthcare

"I have taken opportunities that come my way and embraced them, letting myself be vulnerable and trying things that maybe I wouldn't have tried."

SARAH R.

- Forty-five, two children, single
- New York City-based Model, corporate marketing, entrepreneur

"I rather did my life in reverse, achieving a lot, getting a lot, accomplishing a lot. Then after having kids and getting a divorce and having my own company, I'm realigning myself and I'm re-describing myself... and now trying to reenter my life where I jumped off."

The Working Woman's GPS:
When the Plan to Have It All Has Led You Astray

SHARON

- Fifty-two, three children, single
- Merchandising, lactation consultant, owner of a health food store

"I started [working] at a health food store and eventually opened my own store and that really opened up who I was. It opened my spirituality. I just could not get enough of it, and I could not soak up enough information about herbs, healing, and spirituality and every aspect of the body. . . . My advice to the next generation is: Be true to you. It's one little line I've always said to my kids even when they were little: just be true to yourselves. And even when something seems impossible or against the grain they really have to look inside and say 'Is this going to make me happy?' and if not, no matter how difficult it is, you have to change it, otherwise, you're going to be miserable. You have to be true to yourself; you have to be honest with yourself if you're going to be happy."

SHELLEY

- Forty, married, two children
- Software expert, High Tech

"I'm a creative person and I like gardening and pottery and being outside. So I really want a future that includes a creative side, lets me be outside, and gives me the unlimited time requirement and flexibility to do what I want—that's important to me. ... And I also want to really be able to spend time with my kids at their school right now. They're young. They want me in their classrooms doing stuff for the class. They want to see me there. It's a constant battle of guilt and job commitments. Something's gotta give, all the time. It can't always be your family that gives. So you really have to prioritize what's important for both your career and your family and try to have things fit together and meet somewhere in the middle."

ADDENDUM B:
THE COMMUNITY [BLOG]

You can find me at:
www.JJDiGeronimo.com.

One of my dreams for this book is to be a catalyst for conversation throughout the world, to have a place where women can come together both virtually and in person to learn, guide, empower, support, and celebrate one another as we all strive to create lives of inspiration.

1 LIFE, 1 GOAL, 1 YOU

1 GOAL: Be the best you can be in this lifetime since there is only 1 of you that can make the difference you were brought here to make.

It Is Time!

Acknowledgments

Thank you to my children who have shown me what it means to be truly selfless, who have guided me toward lessons that I never knew I needed to learn and who have presented life in a way I forgot to acknowledge. I hope this book will one day give you permission, if you need it, to live the life you were meant to live, following your inner drive, and making the impact you were brought here to make.

Thank you to my Husband with whom I have no beginning, no end, just a continuation that has fostered a launch pad full of love, acceptance, and encouragement.

Thank you to my Family whose unconditional love has been a guiding light and safe haven for growth.

Thank you to my Friends who have been there for me—you know who you are—and for the bonds we have that are deep and wide.

Thank you to all the women who consented to be interviewed, to all the women who have come together to form Tech Savvy Women, and to all the women who come together to share, celebrate, and guide.

A special thank you to Deborah Burke who played an important role in getting my ideas ready for publication; to Deborah Chaddock Brown who has shared her social media expertise and creative voice; to Patty Penca who has brought the book and blog to life with her creative designs; and, to Patricia M. Gerkin who was my final editor. Working with you all was such a wonderful part of the journey.

www.ingramcontent.com/pod-product-compliance
Lightning Source LLC
Chambersburg PA
CBHW060508130626

46553CB00002B/436